Inspiration from Girl, Walk With Me

Penda L. James challenges us to be transparent in our faith walk with God. She boldly reassures us that nothing or no one can pluck us from God's hands. This is a must read.

---Rev. Dr. Mary L. Buckley | Pittsburgh, PA

Penda L. James has shown us over and over again that her writing style calls us to be accountable and calls us to be GREAT! Penda has a heart to encourage people to pursue their dreams and be who God called them to be. You will feel her injecting you with hope and coaching you to the victory of giving birth to your book, business, or whatever dreams that have been instilled within you from GOD. When Penda writes she pours out love and you can truly feel her spirit through her words and thoughts that GOD is all over it! I think about the things I have gone through in my life, and reading this book has made HEALING visible again! Accountability is what you need in difficult seasons of life…you need someone to WALK with you until you can get back to walking with God! As you develop your faith, write your declaration and you can practice reciting it. As people we forget our purpose when we have to endure through struggles and hardships, experience the pain and suffering of heartache, or grieve the loss of loved ones. When we have relationship issues we can tend to move away from God. If you are going through a difficult season, JUST KEEP WALKING! God has not forgotten about you.

---Shantal "Peaches" Cabell | Lexington, Kentucky

Girl, Walk with Me inspires readers to open their minds to create connections in places, with people and through means, which may not have existed otherwise. In a world where relationship with God seems non-existent, this book takes you on a journey through His Word by way of Penda's enlightening anecdotes and personal narratives.

--- Kelley Johnson | Pittsburgh, PA

For my Warrior Mommy who is an example of walking without fear.

*And I give unto them eternal life; and they shall never perish, **neither shall any man pluck them out of my hand.** ---John 10:28 (KJV)*

Girl, Walk with Me: Unpluckable Faith and Accountability
Copyright © 2015 by Penda L. James
ISBN 13: 978-0-9792385-7-4
ISBN10: 0-9792385-7-9
February 2016
Published by: InSCRIBEd Inspiration, LLC.
Pittsburgh, PA

Printed by Lightning Source
Book Layout & Design by Lance Oditt | www.lanceoditt.com
Author Photo: Stephanie Davis

Italics in Scripture references are used for author emphasis only. All scriptures reference the Kings James Version of the Bible unless otherwise noted.

Join InSCRIBEd Inspiration Online
Website: http://www.unpluckablefaith.com

Twitter: @penscribed

Facebook Group: https://www.facebook.com/groups/GirlWalkwithMe/

Girl, Walk With Me

Unpluckable Faith and Accountability

Penda L. James

Acknowledgments

Everybody is not meant to take every journey with you. ---Norméa Banner

I believe there is truth in the African Proverb, "*I am because WE are. WE are because I am.*" There are people too numerous to thank for my position in life and success as an author. I am grateful to have a family who sees me and calls me to greatness.

I need to give public appreciation to the following individuals who made this project tangible:
• I am grateful for Dr. LaShonda Fuller, Kelley Johnson, Khadijah Pettus, Lyndell Robinson, Rodney and Ebony Broussard for their editorial and honest feedback. Their input took this book to higher heights for me and for you.
• Lance Oditt has again broken barriers with his graphic design expertise. I am glad to have a brother in creativity that can help me manifest my thoughts visually.

My adversities have taught me that through conflict it is important to learn what you are truly made of: I am made of strong roots and those family and friends who surround me won't let me fail.

Still Walking,

2016

Girl, Walk With Me
Unpluckable Faith and Accountability

Girl, Walk with Me

Penda, I'm so sorry I haven't been in touch with you but I've been in a cave. A conversation with a friend turned to her outlining the barrage of negative situations that had occurred in her life since we had spoken last. "I've been feeling overwhelmed, angry and frustrated with all the stuff that has been happening in my life." As she kept talking, the real truth came out, "You know what? I was ashamed to call you because I thought you would be mad at me?"

"Mad at you for what?"

"Because I haven't done anything I promised I would do to start my business." There it was, the truth. She released those words and I think she felt free! "I mean, yeah, I had all those other things going on but I just haven't done anything I am supposed to be doing. I gave you my word."

"That's okay," I told her, ruminating on the image of her sitting in a cold, dark cave hiding from me in shame. I understood what it meant when people would see me and turn the other way. "You didn't make those promises to me. You made them to yourself with me as your witness. All I can do is call your name so that you know I am here. When you are ready to try again, let me know, I will walk with you."

When someone chooses me to hold them accountable, I take that seriously. To walk with someone means that I must first love them using I Corinthians 13 as my model and I must agree with them as Amos 3:3 says, "how can two walk together unless they agree?" They must recognize that I can only operate in my ability, which is not greater than God's ability. I try not to take responsibility for a person's goal whether they accomplish it or not, even when I feel the depth of their hopes. Here are a few other things I do when asked to hold someone accountable:

    1.) I pray for, and with them, especially if the goal is not realistic or tangible
    2.) When necessary, either encouragement, support, asking questions or giving an unapologetic push to move toward the goal when they want to quit will be my declaration to them
    3.) Whatever they choose to do, (remain stagnant or act), I operate with love

In the Bible there are examples of people who literally went into a cave. The reasons for this form of a retreat ranged from people hiding in a strong tower for protection, mourning, to escape hardship, burials and some for restoration. The concept of being in a cave has some validity even though I had never heard anyone define shame for not pursuing a personal goal as being in a cave. There are times when a person may need to take a retreat into a figurative "cave" and just like when supporters will surround the cave and see the Lazarus miracle of goals restored.

When my friend explained that she was in a cave, the imagery was so poignant to me that I started to listen to other people around me when they would disappear for periods of time. Some were isolating themselves to regain focus while most of the others were pulling away from me and other friends because they were ashamed about not taking any action on their goals. There is a proverb that illustrates this point for us, *Proverbs 13:12.* *"Hope deferred maketh the heart sick but, when the desire cometh, it is a tree of life."* So even the Bible says, when dreams come true at last, joy comes. My relationships with people who have asked me to hold them accountable are often cyclical. There is always excitement when the goal is shared, celebration when action steps are achieved, disappointment from setbacks and sometimes periods of silence while the other party is re-evaluating their goal. The chart below is how I visualize the cycle.

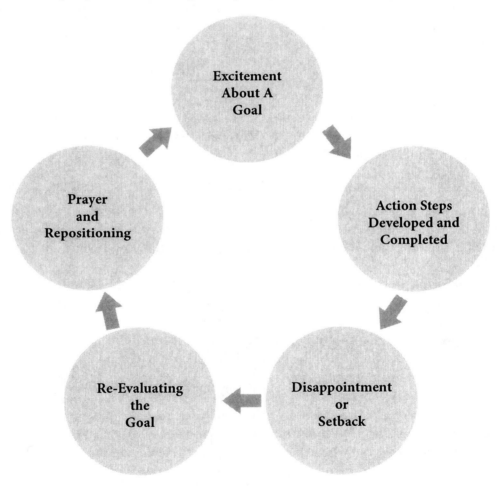

My personal desire is to help people do more in faith, share more of their testimony, and take more risks. God has given everyone the gift of volition; a person can choose to accept or reject their destiny. I am not designed to help them complete the goal; it takes the faith of the *Goal Seeker* to carry the responsibility for their God-given purpose. God has to be the foundation, not pleasing anyone other than Him.

As and accountability partner, my role is to lead them back to Christ, remind them to stand on their Unpluckable Faith and celebrate successes. It has always been helpful to know, in my own experiences, that someone could remind me of my hopes when I could not speak for myself. As long as I remember their goal, I can remind them of it when they forge Only what we do for Christ will last.

Jesus had the disciples to help Him do His work.
Moses had Aaron and Hur to hold up his arms.
Ruth had Naomi to mentor her about Boaz.
Noah had his sons to help him build the ark.
Who do you have to support you in your journey of being God's best?

Girl, Walk With Me. This phrase has many potential meanings and interpretations. The first thing that comes to my mind is God whispering in my ear, *"Penda, I've got you. Just walk."* When I am learning how to walk in new situations, I hear the consistent nudging of the Holy Spirit directing me and guiding my steps. Stumbling and making mistakes are not difficult for babies learning to walk, they don't get embarrassed and ashamed when they fall. I don't know when the paradigm shifted for me, but I believe there is purity in the process a child experiences when learning to walk. I recently overheard a mother say, "When my baby was learning to walk she always looked back to see if I was there." Did all people learning to walk look back to see if someone was there? Are they looking back for safety or accolades? There may be no answer to this question, however, when learning something new, falling down and getting up is part of the process.

Let's think more about a child who is learning to walk. Adults usually keep a close watch on them in case they stumble. I remember that falling was rightening for my daughter. She did not like it at all. With practice, she mastered the skill, walking became easier and confidence in her walk grew until she pulled away from us to walk unassisted. *Goal Seekers* do the same things as children learning to walk: they lean on accountability, master the skill of walking and pull away from the accountability partner or mentor to walk on their own.

I think it is comical to watch a toddler walking between two adults. When the child reaches up to grab the hand of the people walking with them, I imagine that gesture as their way of saying, "walk with me." As the toddler marches, the adults fall in line with the rhythm and pace of their little leader. If the adults walk too fast they could accidentally cause the child to drag behind them. If this happens, all three of them stop walking until the child is back in position. When our daughter was learning to walk, we had to fall in line with her which meant we had to sometimes bend our bodies over so that she could stand up straight.

We took every precautionary measure possible for the protection of our daughter when she was learning to walk. We, were new parents and people often laughed that we would carry the biggest bottle of hand sanitizer we could find, call and check on her at daycare and when she was learning to walk we built human walls for her to walk into so she would not fall. We had safety gates to protect her from stairwells even though we did not have stairwells. Floors were swept to prevent her from eating things she may have found, sharp corners on furniture were covered to shield her from dangerous head bumps. We covered every outlet in the house, even the ones out of her reach. Our senses and the senses of adults in our circle were heightened on her behalf. My husband was always ready to catch her if she leaned over too far or fell. As protectors we were always ready to pick her up and reposition her if she ventured in the wrong direction. I believe that God has precautionary measures in place to protect His children. Do you know the story of Balaam and his donkey? Even though Balaam was trying to do something that God told him not to do, his donkey saw the angel of the Lord and tried to protect him. In Numbers chapter 22 verse 28 it reads, "*And the Lord opened the mouth of the ass, and she said unto Balaam, What have I done unto thee, that thou hast smitten me these three times?*" Just as a parent protects a child from danger, our heavenly father protects His children (*Numbers 22:28, KJV*).

This book is written for both the one cultivating Unpluckable Faith, and for tending your Unpluckable Faith Community. *Girl, Walk with Me* will help you understand when to let people know you need help.

As you build your Unpluckable Faith Community, others cannot be responsible for what God has called **you** to do. No one can do what you are called to do but you. People cannot confirm or deny God's goal for you; it is their responsibility to be a sounding board when you need to give an answer for not taking action. When you want to quit or if you have experienced a setback, this person (or group of people) will remind you of God's promises to you, your pledges to God and to yourself. In some ways they build walls to protect you from danger, or are used by God to pick you up and move you in a different direction.

For every person who has the ability to walk (both physically and spiritually) they have taken steps, experienced falls and gotten back up to walk again. As a member of an Unpluckable Faith community, I don't believe that you can care about someone, see them slipping into trouble and let them slide into disaster when you have it in your power to extend a helping hand. Although a *Goal Seeker* may have to hear negative comments from other people who do not understand their purpose or goals, they will feel "at home" when they talk to you.

> For every person who has the ability to walk, both physically and spiritually) they have taken steps, experienced falls and gotten back up to walk again.

Even if you, as a *Goal Seeker* or member of an Unpluckable Faith Community---may never say the exact words, "*Girl, Walk With Me,*" at some point you will have to ask for help. There will be seasons that happen to all of us: death of loved ones, failure, health crises, financial strain, family problems, and schisms with friends. On your job, at church or even in your home you are not designed to do everything, asking for help is one way of saying, "*Girl, Walk With Me.*" Even though you may believe that you have no fear, it is always good to know that you have the ability to reach out to someone who can pray for you, cry with you, hug you, encourage you or just be present when you don't want to be alone.

Are you a person who prefers to do things on your own because you are a perfectionist and cannot relinquish control? I want you to think about how much stronger you would be if you let the people who love you support you. I hope you will be able to verbalize what you need from your Unpluckable Faith Community. God will never leave us, forsake us or fail us. In one of his final acts, Jesus placed his mother into the care of the disciple John before He died. Have you considered his reason for doing that? Maybe he didn't want her to walk through her grief alone.

I hope you will be able to verbalize to the people who love you, what you need from them when you walk through changing seasons in your life.

Throughout *Girl, Walk with Me*, I have included thought-provoking questions to help you develop a plan of action to walk with Unpluckable faith and accountability. In Part I, you will read about people who have built their faith on an Unpluckable foundation. These testimonies of faith are meant to remind you that faith in God plus your action equals great potential for God to use you. Part II is designed to help you and your Unpluckable Faith Community know what fruit to look for in your relationship. Are you ready to get started? It is time to either come out of your cave or get in position to help someone else strengthen his or her Unpluckable Faith.

Girl, walk with me.

Penda's Declaration of Unpluckability

I am Unpluckable.
God knew me before I was formed in my Mother's womb.
My steps are ordered.
My life is ordained.
I have a specific calling that is sealed in God's hands.

Call me chosen and anointed.
My life is Necessary.
I take risks and choose to be daring.
For that, I am Yare – ready to soar.

I am Unpluckable:
Not easily derailed by life's challenges
Standing on a firm foundation of strength and
I have a mentality of faith that keeps me focused.
I will pursue my goals with intentional tenacity.

No matter what happens, I am Unpluckable.
Strong. Ready. Unwavering.
I will at times be shaken but never shall I be uprooted.
I am in the palm of God's hand.
I am unpluckable.

Scripture References for Girl, Walk With Me

Girl, Walk With Me
Psalms 37:4 | _Delight thyself also in the Lord: and he shall give thee the desires of thine heart._

The Heart of Amani
I Samuel 16:14 | _But the spirit of the Lord departed from Saul, and an evil spirit from the Lord troubled him._

I Samuel 16:23 | And it came to pass, when the evil spirit from God was upon Saul, that David took a harp, and played with his hand: so Saul was refreshed, and was well, and the evil spirit departed from him.

Go Home
Proverbs 27:17 | Iron sharpeneth iron; so a man sharpeneth the countenance of his friend.
The Book of Ruth in its entirety

See the Vision
Proverbs 3:5-6 | Trust in the Lord with all thine heart; and lean not unto thine own understanding. In all thy ways acknowledge Him and He will direct thy paths.

Galatians 6:9 | And let us not be weary in well doing: for in due season we shall reap, if we faint not.

Be Resilient
Psalms 139:14 | I will praise thee; for I am fearfully and wonderfully made: marvelous are they works; and that my soul knoweth right well.

John 10:28 | And I give unto them eternal life; and they shall never perish, neither shall any man pluck them out of my hand.

Stand Through Her Pain
Romans 8:28 | And we know that all things work together for good to them that love God, to them who are the called according to his purpose.

Don't Give Up On Her
John 10: 8-10 | All that ever came before me are thieves and robbers: but the sheep did not hear them. I am the door: by me if any man enter in, he shall be saved, and shall go in and out, and find pasture. The thief cometh not, but for to steal, and to kill, and to destroy: I am come that they might have life, and that they might have it more abundantly.

Evaluate Your Preconceptions
Proverbs 18:21 | Death and life are in the power of the tongue: and they that love it shall eat the fruit thereof.

Roots:
WHAT IS UNPLUCKABLE FAITH?

Rock the World?

Penda, listen to me! She sounded frustrated. I had gotten myself into a conflict with my friend Jaki because I was not listening to her. If she had called at any other time I might have given her my full attention but at that time, I was drained from a long day of work. Jaki had been without a phone for several months and I had to wait until she called me to hear how she was doing. None of our mutual connections had seen or heard from her and I was trying not to worry about her well-being. Usually she would emerge with grandeur like a phoenix from ashes. I was on my way to bed when she called but because I had not seen, or spoken to her for several months it was important to hear where Jaki's life had taken her.

When Jaki was emerging from that season of silence on that particular day I did not feel like talking. My energy was depleted and my daughter's energy was magnified. It was our bedtime and talking on the phone was the last thing I wanted to do. When I saw it was her calling, I thought I was going to hear Jaki's voice, make sure she was okay and call her back another time. Unfortunately, Jaki's living arrangement dictated when she was able to talk on the phone; there was no way to know when Jaki would be able to call me again.

There was so much she wanted to share and she was talking so quickly that I couldn't keep up. If Jaki had written me a letter I might have responded differently to the news that she had been living in a women's shelter with her son. I might have cried thinking about how everything my sister had worked for was reduced to a curfew and a cot infested with bedbugs. I was in a daze thinking about what she was saying but not really hearing it. Jaki was probably talking for a long time and had stopped to ask me a question. I heard her say, "Penda, listen to me!"

"I'm here. I heard you say you were living with recovering drug addicts and former inmates." I let Jaki talk some more while I really tried to listen to her. There was so much going on around me. The volume was loud on the television and that effected how my daughter was laughing – loudly. I think while Jaki was talking I got caught up in the cartoons too. I was sitting on the couch with the phone to my ear while staring at the dust on the ceiling fan. I had so many distractions surrounding me and to top it all of the soothing sound of the ceiling fan was lulling me into a relaxed state.

"God is using me to be a blessing to the women in the shelter." She sounded so happy, "I have been talking to these women. I am learning a lot from them and I am able to minister to them." I added some commentary, "It's great that you can tell other people about the love of Christ when this is such a difficult time for you."

"We are having some life-changing conversations." She was still talking about her time with the other women, "I could never imagine anyone going through some of the things I heard them talk about." Jaki shared how God had transformed her housemates and that the stories of the women gave her continued hope. "God is going to restore me Penda. I am going to get everything He has for me." She was excited to tell me their stories and then I heard her say, "I want to write an anthology."

"Okay. I can help you." I love anthologies, how could I turn her down? I was giving a few comments to play the part of a good listener but I was not tuned in to the conversation. She wanted confirmation of my commitment to help her publish her book, "You will help me publish this anthology?"

"Yes. This sounds like a great idea." That seemed to satisfy her for a minute. I must have reverted back to my daze of distraction. I heard Jaki say again, Penda are you listening?" "I can send you a little money but I don't get paid until Friday." My daughter was being a gymnast on the couch, "Baby, stop doing that!"

Jaki was upset, "I didn't ask you for no money!" I could hear her sigh, "I know you have a family." *Oh. Where did that come from?* I thought to myself. I wanted to support Jaki and I thought she needed money. If I had not been so distracted I would have understood immediately that Jaki was content staying in the shelter temporarily. She was looking for God to work a miracle in her life. Jaki is the type of person who can find the work of God in anything. Because we attended the same church and worked together closely we developed a relationship like blood sisters. When she yelled at me to listen to her, I had to get myself together. Jaki has been my friend for over twenty years. Because we are part of each other's Unpluckable Faith Communities, there is no mincing of words if something is being done that is annoying or out of character by either party.

When Jaki arrested my attention with her commandment to listen to her, she made me look into my own "I" - the reality of my own testimony. She went back to talking about her book, "I have a title for it already." I liked the idea but kept interrupting her to interject my own values. I was trying to make the raw experiences of Jaki and her new friends fit into a nice Christian box with scriptures and pretty bows. "My curfew is almost here. I don't have much time to talk. Listen to me!" I awoke from what felt like a deep slumber. I became fully aware of my attitude, judgments and personal experiences. I sat up straight so I could hear clearly what was being communicated to me.

"You can't ignore the facts of what has happened to these women. They need to hear from God too."

Jaki was right in her statement. For me to ignore the reality of what had happened in these women's lives was to continue to ignore countless women who are stereotyped and rejected. Jaki was creating a voice for this group of women and she was finding her own voice. Jaki was encouraging me not to judge these women before hearing the whole story. "If you have never walked in their shoes you won't understand their "I" story. If you do not listen you will always be judgmental."

The truth of her declaration arrested my attention. "I'm sorry Jaki." I uncrossed my arms, stood up to turn off the fan and sat up straight on the couch. I closed my eyes to become fully present with Jaki, "I promise. I am listening." I knew she was sitting outside so I imagined we were sitting on the curb. I knew Jaki had taken a walk to get some privacy, the sound of buses and cars helped me envision the area where she was sitting. I could hear her inhaling and exhaling her cigarette through the phone. I imagined her white French-tipped fingernails scratching through the air as she spoke with smoke trailing behind.

Jaki was animated while talking about her idea. She was jumping from one person to another, telling me about the people she had met and the lessons she learned from them. She would mention a name and I would try to visualize the woman by her descriptions. At that point I was actively listening and trying to repeat what I heard her say so she knew I was engaged. "One is called Pretty Princess you say?" "She is so pretty Penda. Her skin is chocolate and her daughter has long hair. I met this other young girl whose mother gave her illegal drugs when she was young. As if on cue, my child crawled into my lap and began to give me kisses on my forehead. That imagery of a mother sitting down and sharing drugs with her child gave me chills.

Jaki shared how her new friend vowed to never allow anything to happen to her daughter. That blows my mind Penda." My mind was open too. I could not help but think about all of the times God had protected me. I started to reflect on my own parents their expressions of love to me. My mind recalled the scripture in Romans chapter 8 verses 38 and 39 that says "nothing can separate us from the love of God." I was thankful. My "I story" was coming to me.

"Think about it Penda." Jaki was teaching me again, "Even though we may not have had the extreme testimonies of some of the women I have met, we have our own "I's." "What do you mean by that?" I was curious.

"These women are survivors. Don't you realize that when you tell your survivor story you start with the phrase "I was . . .?" I thought about that and mentally agreed. "The "I" statements we speak are the autobiographical statements and mind blowing testimonies that remind us how far God has brought us. If people knew these women's stories, it would rock the world. We need to tell our 'I stories' so other people can get free!"

Rock the world. The vibration of that statement has stayed with me. What can I do to teach people to press through their pain to the promise? How can I encourage people to put their faith over their fear? What about reminding people about the reality of God's grace after a purpose has been aborted? This is what I desire to do on a daily basis. Because I was able to listen to Jaki, I recognized that I try to find ways to help women see that they are not alone in their pain. I was already doing what Jaki was trying to do; she was asking to partner with me so she could walk in her own path of encouraging others.

As you reflect on your goals, imagine the strength of a ladybug that held on to a dandelion seed and flew through the air into its new season. The ladybug was content to hold on and fly with no idea where it would land. How much faith do you have? Can you hold on and trust where God is taking you? You do not have to do anything to be Unpluckable; you just are, hold on and get ready for your faith ride! The key points to remember from this chapter are for you to teach your Unpluckable Faith Community (or accountability partner) how to respond to you when you need them and they are not fully engaged.

There are several things that Jaki did when I was not listening to her:

1. She commanded my attention with strong words when she knew I was not listening to her. Because she needed me in that moment, she told me specifically what she wanted me to do to assist her.

2. She pointed out when I was acting out of character and how that was affecting her in the moment.

3. Jaki heard my judgmental statements toward her new friends; she put a mirror in front of me so that I could reflect on my own testimony of getting back up after a fall. She reminded me that God worked in my life in a different way.

4. Jaki stood her ground on her goal for the anthology. When I tried to change the message from the raw reality of the women she had met, Jaki refused to allow me to take away the authenticity of their experiences. She knew what she wanted and would not accept what I wanted for her.

5. Jaki called me to check in, she did not want anything but to talk. I offered her money and she quickly addressed my misunderstanding of her needs. Even though she could have used money, she was trusting God to supply all of her needs.

There may be times that you will have to yell out to your Unpluckable Faith Community, "Hold up! I can't walk that fast," or "I'm not supposed to go that way!" Just like the toddler learning to walk, the adults walking with the child know when to slow down so they don't drag the baby behind them, you will not allow yourself to be dragged when you have your Unpluckable Faith rooted in God like a dandelion. Help your Unpluckable Faith community understand your position, be confident, and speak with assurance of your purpose. You are yare (ready), rock the world and we are waiting to hear your "I" story!

Tending the Roots of Unpluckable Faith

What would it look like if you had one chance to "Rock the World?"

The Heart of Amani

I was disappointed when Terra told me she had to close her coffee shop. So disappointed — I think I cried. Outside circumstances including the lack of consistent customers is what forced Amani to be laid to rest after six years of being open. My grief was in no way comparable to what its owner, Terra may have felt. Not only did I have lunch at Amani a few times a week, the coffee shop had been my lunch escape for two years. I met some great people there and on my lunch breaks was able to meet with many of my first Scribe clients. What did the closing of Amani mean for me?

I don't remember who introduced me to the place or helped me find it but I am forever grateful; this was a divine connection. I could travel to Amani from my job within seven minutes. I was able to have an escape from the drama of the office and my child welfare cases in an atmosphere that was positive and empowering. Going to the coffee shop was like going to a friend's house in the middle of the work day. Usually there was music playing from the inside that greeted me on the sidewalk when I got out of my car. The tunes would lure me inside where Terra always welcomed me with a smile and always had music on rotation, which soothed my soul. I don't drink coffee but my soul's thirst was quenched at Amani. Maybe that is how King Saul felt when David played the lyre for him *(I Samuel 16:14, KJV)*. I would leave Amani refreshed and full literally and spiritually.

The first time I visited Amani I remember taking mental notes about the beautiful decor I wanted to replicate in my house: orange paint on the walls, curtain dividers, stools and low sitting coffee tables. I had a vision board of cut outs of those same items! Amani coffee shop was a hidden gem on Tripoli Street and when I met Terra I was proud of her accomplishment. I recognized that Terra was the owner immediately; the photos of her family on the wall and the numerous newspaper articles highlighting her accomplishments were evident that she was in charge.

I was ecstatic to see a young African American woman on fire in the entrepreneurial world, especially in the Pittsburgh area. I was intentional to learn about Terra's goals. I tried to network with her to keep myself motivated to pursue my goals. She supported me by allowing me to attend poetry readings and host book signings at Amani.

One of the things I would miss about Amani was that it was like my office. Amani was a safe space, like a cocoon for many of my first coaching clients to be nurtured. One Scribe in particular was emotionally and creatively broken. We met once a week, sat at the same table and I would eat a chicken Panini and drink peach tea while she talked. Eventually she was able to not only write her testimony for publication but she read it aloud at Amani! Even though she hid her face behind her book, sat in a chair and was visibly shaken, this author conquered her fear of public speaking. By the time Amani closed, my former client was a woman with renewed confidence. She is now a workshop presenter.

It is interesting that one meaning of the word Amani is "wishes." When Terra and I spoke after Amani had closed, our conversation led me to think deeply about knowing when to stop giving cardio pulmonary resuscitation to a dying dream and let it pass peacefully. I wondered is *everything I desire to do really God's desire for me*? Is everything you desire to do God's desire for you? This is a hard question to ask, but if you are going to keep walking after a failure, you have to be honest about your why. Why did you do this in the first place? What did you love about it? Did you really love it? If you have no explanation for the why, you may need to rethink your desire for that goal.

I understand through the closing of Amani that seasons change. Not soon after I left the job on that side of town is when Amani closed. As it had nurtured my former client, it had given me "home" when I needed a reprieve from the job. I was thankful Amani was there when I needed it, and I was happy to see that Terra had found something new to bring her joy. The heart of Amani is the root of our wishes.

As a *Goal Seeker* where is the heart of your passion? Find your why so you can keep walking toward the completion of it. If you are leaning on something that needs to be laid to rest put it down so you can pick up your feet and walk again. A conversation with someone in your Unpluckable Faith Community could possibly bring some things into perspective for you. Take some time to ponder your wishes, and make sure your desires are in line with what God wants for you. If your will and God's will are not aligned, lay your wishes to rest.

Tending the Roots of Unpluckable Faith

Have you ever had a dream or a goal that you had to lay to rest? If you have, why and what was it?

Where Are You?

Hi Friend. Where are you right now? Are you sitting at your desk at work or are you sitting on the couch reading this book? Maybe you are snuggled under a blanket or riding in a car on your way to a special destination. Where are you right now literally? *Think about it . . .*

An *Eco-Map* is used in several different capacities to illustrate systems and how they are related to one another. It is a variation of several different types of eco-maps and genograms that I have seen used in the past. In a dream, I saw myself being pulled in several directions and I was trying to decide where I was supposed to go next. It reminded me of something my friend Dallas once lamented, *"How can I be complete when everyone wants a piece of me?"*

My Eco-Map

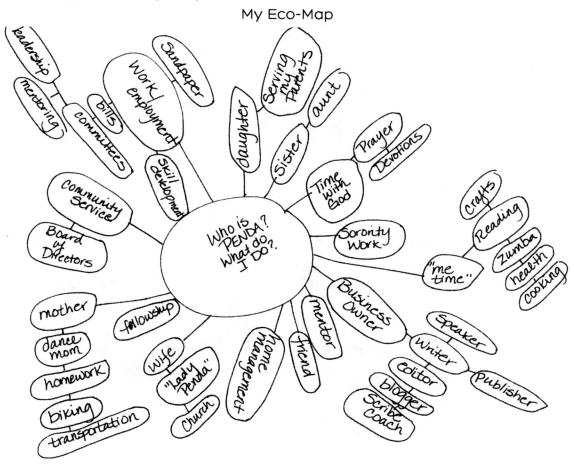

When I woke from the dream, I pondered everything I needed to put on my list as I looked for my journal. I felt tense in my shoulders and I was astounded at how much responsibility I was thinking about at the time.. By the time I was able to sit down and draw my picture, I had only two colored highlighters and a pen. I saw that most of my self is tied to my family life but I also have a responsibilities with my service organizations. When I added one thing to the list it let me to think about another thing, which led me to something else. When I finished my drawing my breathing changed. Seeing the commitments on paper showed me where I was unbalanced, and needed to let some things go. The picture gave me a better idea of how to work on my schedule to build in time for myself. Helped me recognize "*YES!, I have time for myself.*" If I do, so do you!

When I did this exercise with my mentee I was overwhelmed by her drawing. It was a lot for me to see and I could not imagine how she could live this reality. We thought of ways to delegate responsibilities to other people at work, church and in her personal life. We were able to create a way for her to give herself permission to take a break when she needs to get refreshed. My mentee is busy, but she also needs to rest. It was interesting to me that she colored every part of her picture except her own name. That oversight showed us that she makes everyone else a priority. When I pointed it out to her, she realized her tendency to do this to herself and thus we created a self-care plan. Her Drawing:

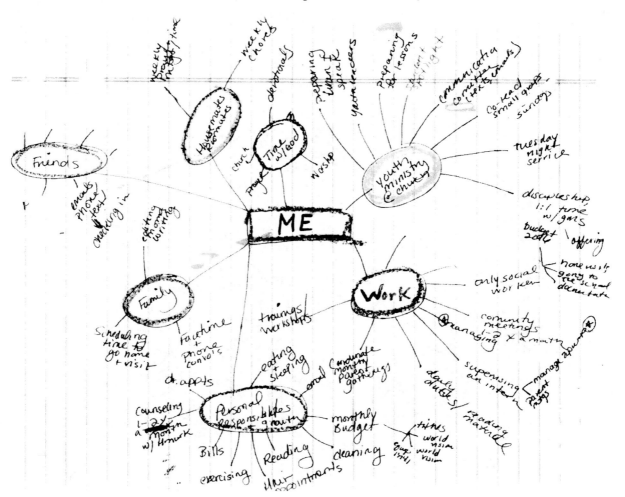

Girl, Walk With Me | Unpluckable Faith and Accountability

Are you prone to put others before yourself so much that you forget your own needs? If so, stop that behavior immediately. Getting your goals accomplished is possible and the time is available to you if you are looking for it. You may be busy and you may have a lot of responsibilities, however you have to take the time to take care of yourself and your temple. Exercise, eat healthy foods, talk to a friend, there are many things you can build into your "to do list" to help keep you on track. If you think about where you are right now it will be easier to make a plan to get where you want to be.

Once you see how you walk and where you walk, maybe it will help you understand why you feel overwhelmed at times. When you can verbalize how others can help you, this is one big step in building your Unpluckable Faith Community.

CREATING YOUR OWN ECO-MAP

1. Draw a cirlce in the center of a blank piece of paper and put your name in it.
2. Draw a line from your self and create a new circle. In that second circle
   add a responsibility or commitment.
3. Continue drawing lines and circles until you have mapped all your obligations.

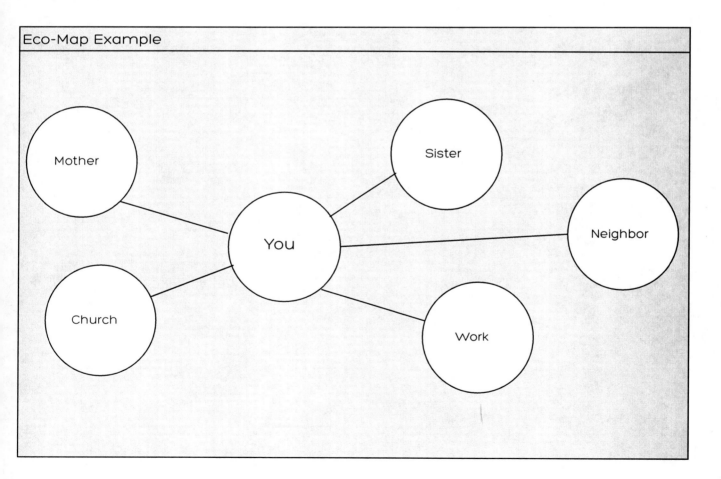

Eco-Map Example

MY ECO-MAP
Using the space below, create your own Eco-Map and then answer the questions on the following page. If you think you will need more space, flip the page side ways, or use a blank piece of paper.

What are some things you can let go of to give yourself a break?

What is the motivating factor to help you complete a goal you have in process right now?

Go Home

Every time I hear Stephanie Mills' version of the song "Home" from the 1978 movie *The Wiz* it brings tears to my eyes. The song, reminds me to honor and respect those people and experiences in my life that have taught me the hardest lessons. The words to the song parallel my belief about what I find in my safe places with family, friends, accountability partners and mentors. The main character experiences gets lost in an unknown land and has to overcome several obstacles to get the wisdom she needs to return to her family. She meets friends who are on their own quest for knowledge and together they grow in maturity. As the story concludes, Dorothy begins to yearn for her home and sings a song to express her dream to return there. Some of what Dorothy sings about is important to me: love, familiarity, and family. Like Dorothy I may have gotten lost, but I have always found my way "home."

When I lose balance and get deflated by my failures "home" is a safe place for me to lie down and cry until I heal. In this space, with people who care about me (friends, family members, and prayer partners) I can allow my tears to express my feelings when I cannot utter words. People who love me encourage me to be vulnerable and will not allow me to quit. When I hit that proverbial wall that knocks me down I have a safe place where I can be myself. At "home" I am able to recall fond memories, reflect on my personal history, and my reason for pursuing my goals. "Home" is where I can be myself without fear of people judging me. When you face an obstacle, no one will blame you if you go "home" for a strong embrace from a loved one and a soul detox. It is possible to recapture your delight in pursuing your goals, you may need some time to rest before you can start again.

At "home" someone reminds me how precious I am to them, and in the eyes of God. The Bible calls this *Iron Sharpening Iron (Proverbs 27:17, KJV)*. At "home" I am reminded that I am valued and loved unconditionally. Despite my shortcomings or my challenges I can find healing and support at "home." My Great Uncle Marvin would describe "home" as feelin' fine, satisfied and happy. I want to be feelin' fine, satisfied and happy as often as I can.

I have spent time as a mentor to encourage younger people to define and implement their version of success and what it means to be feelin' fine, satisfied and happy. My passion about mentorship is largely due to the number of people in my life who appeared stuck or complacent. I have watched so many of my intimate connections struggle for years with distractions that shifted their focus to something they did not really want to pursue. This is why I believe there are opportunities to restore your power in intentional and positive fellowship with people who will not allow you to hide; they will call you out of your excuses and shame. I have watched people in my life fight low self-esteem, rejection, heartbreak and confusion. I have felt myself getting deeply angry and frustrated about these thieves that have robbed my loved ones of their lives! One way I teach my mentees to counteract these rotten fruit is by cultivating visibility and meeting new people and trying new things. Go be a bridge. Just go do something other than sit and wish you were doing something!

Mentorship with someone who supports your goals can heighten your awareness and expose you to things you could not imagine for yourself. In some ways, this relationship can be "home" for you. There is a Biblical example of an Unpluckable Faith Connection in the form of Ruth and Naomi (*see The Book of Ruth*). In short, Ruth was the daughter-in-law of Naomi, who forsook her home to follow Naomi back to her land, Moab, when her husband and sons suffered untimely deaths. Orpah, Ruth's sister-in-law returned to her homeland but Ruth accepted the covering and mentorship of Naomi and was obedient to her. In chapter 1 verse 16 Ruth told Naomi, "*Where you go I will go.*" She literally walked with her back to where she had originated. Read the story of Ruth and Naomi and write down characteristics of mentorship that you identify. Here are mine:

1. Naomi confirmed Ruth's purpose (Verse 22)
2. Naomi offered wisdom and instruction (Verses 3 and 4)
3. Naomi provided protection (Verse 22)
4. Naomi gave Ruth a place to rest (Verse 23)
5. Naomi saw a way out for her situation and gave her tools (Verse 3:1)
6. Throughout, Naomi showed concern for Ruth's well-being

I will use one of my mentor/mentee relationships from graduate school at Bowling Green State University to highlight how these traits worked for me and how they can work for you.

1. Choose a mentor who will *MODEL* success in the area you are trying to pursue. Being mentored by Carolyn deeply influenced me and through the years has formed my work/life passion (confirmation of purpose). There were many times that Carolyn would ask me, "Why do you think you are responding that way?"

2. Carolyn Brightharp was studying for her Doctorate. I participated in her "Model of Hope and Healing" mentoring program, which was designed for African American women on campus. She invited women who were graduate students, faculty and staff from the university to participate. As a group we had a safe space with one another to discuss articles from magazines and journals and listen to guest speakers with topics relevant to us as women of color (a place to rest). Choose a mentor who will *GIVE* you tasks to complete relative to your current position and how it relates to your goals.

3. As a group we verbalized our goals and discussed the potential glass ceilings that could limit some of us from progressing in our careers. This group was a form of an Unpluckable Faith Community. Carolyn helped us identify barriers and see opportunities to shatter them with the support we had in within the group (concern for one another's well-being, protection, wisdom and instruction).Carolyn taught us the value of self-reflection as an opportunity to foster growth.

4. As my mentor, Carolyn held me to a high standard, often identifying challenges and weaknesses along with strengths. Because she had already earned her Master's degree, she was able to give me tools for success. She edited my thesis and introduced me to individuals in her circle that could support my professional goals. She believed that I was going to be successful and with every benchmark I accomplished Carolyn kept pushing me to improve.

To continue this lesson on the value of mentors let me share with you how mentorship has worked in my career. A few years after graduate school I was employed a small non-profit. My supervisor was younger than I was and we were like oil and water. Never agreeing on anything. In those times, when conflict at work sent me rushing "home" I did not realize she was creating "home" for me at work. This relationship forced me to look at myself as Carolyn had taught me to do. On one particular day Ms. Canada grew frustrated with our clash and locked eyes with me before she quietly said, "Penda, I am your sandpaper." "What does that mean?" I was huffing and looking at her with disdain. I can imagine that my arms were crossed and my wall of defense was up. "I am your supervisor and it is my responsibility to smooth out your rough edges." She paused and took a deep breath, "*Like sandpaper on a piece of wood, that's what I plan to do for you.*"

Hmm. What could I say to that? As much as we clashed, we respected one another. Ms. Canada's sentiment relaxed me; it freed me from the need to fight – she cared about me. The conflict wasn't that we did not like each other; it was that she had identified things that I could improve and like Carolyn, was pointing them out. What I did not like was the identification of my weaknesses, it had nothing to do with my supervisor. Ms. Canada was guiding me out of my comfort zone and I was pugnacious. That statement helped me to let my shield down and listen to her. As a result, I was able to re-frame how I interacted with our consumers and with her.

Ms. Canada had never intended to harm me; she was always giving me insight into myself that I could not see! I believe this is the power of a mentor: they ask you the challenging and critical questions to challenge your thinking. Mentors pour water on your roots so that you have room to grow. When you want to give up, a mentor will massage your character, toughen your leadership abilities, and identify hidden strengths and weaknesses you cannot see. You need both a mentor and, an accountability partner to help you pursue your goals. A mentor will model success and check on your progress. In contrast, an accountability partner will pray for you and listen to your excuses.

You need both a mentor and an accountability partner who will help you pursue your goals by assisting you in creating a plan of action toward achieving them.

Both Carolyn and Ms. Canada gave me tools to be a better person at work and in my personal affairs. If you feel dull maybe you need to have your iron sharpened by a mentor so you can finish your assignment.

What qualities do you need in a mentor?

See the Vision

The Bible tells us that if we acknowledge God in every decision we make He will direct our steps (Proverbs 3:5-6, KJV). Imagine if all of your steps were covered in rose petals. Coming to America is a movie that was released in 1998. If you have seen it you can imagine a line of rose petals that pointed to where Prince Akeem (Eddie Murphy's character) walked. Akeem was from the fictional nation of Zamunda who moved to America looking for a princess to wed. Akeem had a vision to find a wife who would love him authentically. Prince Akeem's assistants walked in front of him and dropped rose petals at his feet, which illuminated his path. Anyone could follow his path because the rose petals Do you think you would walk differently if rose petals were thrown at your feet? Would the rose petals help you see the vision of God's purpose in your life?

For many years I have utilized vision boards to help me see my goals. This is nothing like having rose petals thrown at my feet, but I use vision boards to create short and long term steps for my goals and dreams. The vision board is always taped on the wall somewhere in my house where I can ponder it every day when I see it. I add things to my board as I reevaluate what I want to accomplish. My intention for having a vision board is to articulate to myself what I want to achieve in my life each year. My goals are often focused on my finances, health, spirituality, relationships, or career. Since I started my business, InSCRIBEd Inspiration in 2000 I created business and personal goals individually for the sake of expanding my foresight. In 2012, I merged my vision boards into one, there was a common thread, meeting Maya Angelou.

Although creating a vision board was a great idea, there was a problem in my process. I did not take any action required to meet Maya Angelou. I was looking at her picture every day and not creating steps to convert my dream to meet her into reality. It was possible to meet her through many connections of friends and extended friends, but I was not daring enough to do so. There was no substance behind the pictures, no action being taken to make it happen even though rose petals were already showing me where to walk! All I had was pictures of Maya Angelou glued to a piece of paper. Leads given to me about places she was going to be, friends who had a connection that knew her, or suggestions to send my writing to her publicist were left untended. At every hand I hesitated because I was afraid of failure. I did not do everything I could have done to meet Maya Angelou.

Martha Beck described in her July 30, 2008 blog post, The Subtle Tricks to Building an Effective Vision Board that we have to do more than just create a vision board. I had made a vision board "devoid of real purpose and emotion" (www.marthabeck.com). I spent more time thinking about meeting my hero than

I did trying to encounter her. I had built an altar to my idol instead of building my own legacy. When I started to take action on the goal to meet her, she was already failing in health and had stopped traveling. When she died, I had no one to blame but myself for my shattered dream.

I asked myself---*Maya Angelou has left her mark on the world what are you going to do?* While mourning my dream I began to ponder what I loved about Maya Angelou. She taught me about the responsibility of a writer. My new goal is to nurture the future generation of scribes, to unlock passion and purpose, I see this vision. I will create work that moves people in the way Maya Angelou moved me from my dark space, releasing the latch on my invisible cage. I accepted this goal one morning a few months after her death. I had slipped out of bed around 5 a.m. because I could not sleep. I slowly drooped to the floor in our home office and let myself cry. I was sobbing silently for the sake of my sleeping family, but the tears were necessary for my cleansing. I had watched online as Wake Forest University hosted her life celebration. I had watched many of the television programs honoring her after she died but I could not forgive myself for not doing what I needed to do to meet her. To have seen the vision and not taken action to achieve it was my biggest mistake. I will not allow that to happen again when I attempt to achieve a goal.

On top of Maya Angelou passing away, my mom and Grandma Dear within weeks of each other were given the same alarming medical diagnosis and required surgery. My mother-in-law received news from her doctor that we did not want to hear. It seemed that during that time everything I knew and loved was falling apart. When did I have time to think about my hopes and aspirations?

Emotionally I was fragmented with these heavy circumstances but did not admit my truth. As the oldest child I wanted to be strong for my siblings and everyone who was watching me. I felt alone and discouraged until I allowed myself to cry that morning. Through my tears I acknowledged the meaning of letting go. I absorbed what people meant when they said things like, "Maybe it wasn't meant for you to meet her." Or "Maybe God wants you to leave a message to someone through your writing." Through the release of my tears I quit holding myself hostage and harboring resentment toward myself. I relinquished the blanket of fear about my family's health and that allowed me to see my renewed vision.

Admitting that I had failed in achieving my goal was painful to accept. But I did, I grieved my dream, I picked myself up off of the floor and I began to search for a concrete goal versus a new dream. *How did I get here?* I asked myself that question a number of times but could not create an answer that calmed my emotions. I had quit on myself and chose one thing out of a list of hundreds of goals to emphasize; I failed at that one thing and didn't recognize the numerous other opportunities to accomplish something great with my life. I was telling people that they were Unpluckable but I had forgotten what it meant to follow my deep roots and trust God. I reasoned with myself that I did not need intentional tenacity if my goal no longer existed. But I thank God for my supporters who would not let me be mediocre. They called me, sent text messages, prayed and forced me to verbalize a new goal. Because of them I quit running with my pain and ran to my Heavenly Father who helped me see His vision for me.
I remembered my own words about being Unpluckable. The Unpluckable position is the place where nothing can deter you from your goal. Like a padlock, clamp on to that goal and do not let go of it. When

you hit a barrier practice digging your roots in deep and stand in your Unpluckable position so that you can overcome the setback. When you do not achieve a goal, reevaluate what you could have done differently and create a new strategy, or a new goal. When I recognized my worth and value and began to carry myself with a new standard it forced the people around me to treat me differently because I had created new boundaries.

I re-evaluated my goals and revised the list of where I'm from:

- I'm from unfulfilled goals
- I'm from Phenomenal Woman
- I'm from building a legacy.
- I'm from chasing dreams

As you seek God about your assignment from Him, you may hit proverbial walls that knock you down. I encourage you to be daring, if the goal is from God, He will provide everything you need to accomplish it. Put a timeline on your goals. When you get discouraged, disappointed, and frustrated there will be a sense of urgency reminding you that you have something to finish. As long as you have a support system, they will walk with you to the finish line. If you have recognized that your original goal was unrealistic, find a new goal. If you want it, you will work for it. Keep your vision visible, see it and act on it at all times and operate with integrity.

When you are not in the right position, have the courage to shift including making a move, getting a new job, leaving a bad relationship, choosing a new school, (fill in the blank_____). Could it be that failure or disappointments can give you the fuel you need to find your rightful place? Maybe one of your supporters or mentors can help you answer this question.

Who is walking with you to help you shape your vision? Are you walking with God? Tell your supporters when you get tired. Admit when you want to quit. Be honest with yourself when you get to your destination and realize that you don't want to be there. Change and reflection will be with you as you walk. No matter how tired you get, you have to remember your strength comes from God. Think about the root of the dandelion that we talked about. The root sustains the plant and unless the plant is uprooted it can grow from broken roots. Keep with you a list of declarations so that you can find strength when you grow tired. The Bible instructs us not to get weary in well doing (Galatians 6:9).

Utilize Bible scriptures to help you write your own declarations in your journal or in this book and practice speaking them out loud. When you speak these declarations you are confirming that you see the vision. As you internalize these declarations they will begin to renew your mind.

- *I am the head and not the tail*
- *I am more than a conqueror*
- *I am above, not beneath*

Below are some suggested prayers you can add to your personal prayer list. When you are building your Unpluckable Faith you want to build it on a solid foundation of God's Word, which is the Bible. In doing this, He will teach you what it means to have Unpluckable Faith and what to pray for when you pray.

1. Accountability to God
2. Boldness
3. Courage
4. Favor
5. Partnership

6. Peace
7. Protection
8. Vigor
9. Vision
10. Zeal

Tending the Roots of Unpluckable Faith

Use the space below to write your own prayer of Unpluckable Faith

Here is an example of personal declarations that were written by the participants at the Unpluckable Retreat 2015. Create a few within your Unpluckable Faith Community:

I am breathing.
I am walking.
I am blended, not broken.
I am victorYOUs.
I am hopeful.
I am NOT forgotten.
I am successful.
I am SURE. I am bruised and not broken.
I am renewed!
I am me.
I am AMAZED and AMAZING.
I am refreshed.
I am free to be me.
I am bendable.
I am chosen!
I am living a holy life, walking in my mother's footsteps.
I am free to fly in my purpose.
I am fearless.
I am able through Christ.
I am grateful for the blessing of a renewed faith and no fear.
I am Unpluckable!
I am full of faith.
I am powerful.
I am focused.
I am unveiled.
I am abiding.
I am FREE!!
I am anointed.
I am expanding, extending and stretching to be of God's use beyond my reach. Even with it hurts I won't stop. When it hurts, I won't stop. When people turn against me I will keep going. When others talk about me I will listen only for God's voice. When I am not sure what to do, I know that God does.

Tending the Roots of Unpluckable Faith

Could failure or disappointment can give you the fuel you need to find your rightful place? If so, why?

Be Resilient

Dandelions are hard to kill . If you have a garden or a yard and want to eradicate yourself of dandelions many experts advise that to destroy a dandelion you must stop it at the core of its life: the root. One dandelion growing in a yard or garden has the potential to overtake other plants because their thick roots can choke out seedlings trying to grow with them. Dandelion roots are deep and strong. Like you, they are anointed for a purpose even when people do not understand why they exist.

One writer says when you start the process of removing dandelions it is best to do it at the first sign of them growing. If you soak the soil around a dandelion with hot water it loosens the earth and makes it easy to pull the plant - roots intact. At the early stage of maturity the roots are undeveloped. Have you ever had an idea, shared it with someone and gotten discouraged when they spoke negatively about it? The negative words spoken on your dream are like the hot water drenching the soil around a dandelion. Better Homes and Gardens suggest that once the dandelion is freed from the ground, put the uprooted plant in a plastic bag to suffocate it before it can grow. Let's look at it this way: if you have a vision, share it too quickly, someone could pour water on it to drench it, pull it up from the root, and throw it in a bag to suffocate it before it is discarded forever. This is an example of killing your dream (the premature dandelion) at the first sight of it growing. I would suggest that if you have an idea, hold it close to your heart, pray about it and write it down before you share it with anyone. Hot water can scald the root and the plant could be suffocated but if any part of the taproot is left in the ground a dandelion has the power and potential to regrow from broken roots. Your dream can grow from broken roots. But what happens when Dandelions develop roots in hard to reach places?

The first fruit of Unpluckable faith is *resilience*. If a dandelion flower is plucked from the ground, it will return if the root is not destroyed. You will be pulled and shaken by your circumstances, but as long as you have planted your feet (your roots) on a solid foundation of faith, you will stand in the truth of being Unpluckable. You were designed (*Psalms 139:14, KJV*) to be Unpluckable. You may call it resilient, strong, powerful, and full of faith or even courage - I call it being Unpluckable.

Whatever you call it, living with this quality is an evolution that grows through stages of maturity. I have seen many people that I love wither away from fear and disappointment over bad decisions. I pray that they and other droopy dandelions will live again. With all of the ways that dandelions can be killed, our God is still sovereign and has the final say in our lives.

Ladybugs are attracted to dandelions. Ladybugs and dandelions make a great team; ladybugs eat bugs that destroy plants and preserve the fidelity of dandelions. What kind of things and people are attracted to you and how is the atmosphere changed when you enter a space? In the correct position dandelions are able to transform and influence their environment. Dandelions are hard to miss with their vibrant yellow hue. After a few days, the bright yellow blooms transform into seed heads, and take on the look of a lion's mane.

Webster's Dictionary lists the official and Latin term for the word Dandelion as Taraxacum Officinale, which means "remedy." Because of their ability to grow in difficult soil, dandelion roots soften the earth. Some gardeners will allow dandelions to grow with some of their crops so that they can get nutrients from the roots of the dandelion when the soil is hard or has a rock-like consistency.

Dandelion: *Taraxacum Officinale*

Herbalists suggest that dandelions have healing properties, which purify the bloodstream, gall bladder and digestive system. You can ingest dandelions raw, broil the flowers to make tea or boil the roots to make coffee. Dandelions can be put in salads and the stem of the dandelion can be used as glue. When you understand the purpose of thing and its value, you are more apt to use it in the way it was intended. I would suggest that you take some time to consider your value and seek God about your purpose.

In this section of the book we are going to investigate the fruit of Unpluckable Faith. In the previous section you read about other people and their Unpluckable Faith. You were instructed to keep walking. Now, let's take this walk deeper and investigate the strength of dandelions and how using this plant as an illustration can help you keep walking forward to accomplish your goals.

To many children, dandelions are beautiful flowers. Children can access them and they enjoy picking them in bunches to give to their mothers. One of my friends complained to me about a bouquet of dandelion flowers her daughter gave her as *ugly weeds* We laughed about how the baby ran around the park picking as many dandelions as she could find yelling, "*They are so beautiful!*". Her little hands were so full of dandelions when she brought them to her mother that she had squeezed the stems flat.

She sighed, "What am I going to do with these ugly things?" I explained to Tunisia some of the things I have learned about dandelions. Her daughter ran around the park screaming, "They are so beautiful!"

The child thought of her mother and gave her the beauty she beheld in them. Even though Tunisia was saying to herself, "Why is she giving me these ugly things?" She probably once had found beauty in dandelions herself. Age, time and experience have devalued dandelions in Tunisia's sight. That often happens to us, if we do not consistently return to the source of our strength (in our faith, prayer time, personal meditation fellowship with like-minded people or church attendance we could forget our value over time also. I was intrigued while walking during my lunch break after seeing dandelions growing in strange places. I have seen dandelions grow through cracks in the sidewalk, through brick and up walls. If a dandelion is in this Unpluckable position, you may never get access to the root to destroy it. If someone wanted to destroy you, they would have to tear down the wall to get to you. Things will happen on the surface of the plant that has no effect on the root. God erected a wall of protection on your behalf, you are Unpluckable. That often happens to us, if we do not consistently return to the source of our strength (in our faith, prayer time, personal meditation fellowship with like-minded people or church attendance we could forget our value over time also.

Dandelion roots are deep and strong. Like you, they are anointed for a purpose. Nothing can pluck you out of God's hands. Nothing.

When I became aware of the scripture in *John 10:28 KJV* and understood that nothing can pluck me out of God's hand I began to appreciate the power of dandelions and their roots. Dandelions are a physical representation of what it means to be Unpluckable. I challenge you to take a walk and try to find the evidence of dandelions growing all around you. *Remember: Not one thing. No thing. Nothing can pluck you out of God's hand. Keep walking.*

Tending the Roots of Unpluckable Faith

How is the atmosphere changed when you enter a space?

God Keeps His Promises

On a Friday morning in April 2011 I was forced to stand with deep roots and stretch my Unpluckable Faith. Can you recall a time where you questioned your faith? I want to share one experience and what I learned about trusting God.

My husband and I sat with my daughter and watched cartoons. He was leaving for a business trip that morning and we wanted to have a few minutes of family time. The baby and I were giggling and discussing the show during the trip to the daycare and when we arrived I observed the news van parked across the street. In that neighborhood there was constant news activity taking place to the point where I learned to dismiss their presence. As was my ritual, I got out of the car, touched my forehead to my daughter's head in the back seat and prayed for God to keep our family safe as we went our separate ways. I always ended my prayer with something like, "And Lord, let her have a fun day at school."

We said "Amen," I gave her a kiss and lifted my head to take her out of the car. As I started to unbuckle the seatbelt, I felt a touch on my shoulder; I turned and was greeted by the cameraman and a reporter! "Ma'am, I need to tell you what has been going on inside of your daughter's school." I closed my daughter's car door. Something told me that nothing good was going to come from this conversation. As soon as the door closed my daughter started to scream, "Mommy!" Her unanswered attempts to gain my attention turned into sobs and a temper tantrum. A four year old does not understand silence. She wanted to get out and I did not want her to hear the information relayed to me by the reporter. There had been illicit activity on the daycare grounds. "The director of this daycare was arrested this morning." He was emotionless and pointed the microphone in my face, "What do you think about this Ma'am?"

He was doing his job, but I was in crisis. On the news I looked like a deer in headlights with my eyes wide open and glassy with tears. I stuttered through my dry mouth, "I need to call my husband." I guess that was enough, they rolled the camera until I turned away from the camera and got in the car. While our daughter screamed to get out of the car I called my husband and we created a plan for the day. I called my boss and explained I would be late for training. "I know I can't miss any days of this training . . .," I told him, ". . . but my daughter's daycare was just raided for drugs." I took the baby to my husband who pushed the departure time back for his trip so I could go to work. On my way to him I thought to myself, *She loves school, how do I explain that she can't go back? How do I tell her she won't see her friends again?*

My boss and a few of my coworkers watched the news and by the time I made it to the office people were approaching me in the hall, "Penda, are you okay? How is your daughter? How long has she been there?" They shot inquiries at me like arrows and I was too numb to have long responses, "I'm fine. She's with her father. A year."

I tried to proceed with my day and ignore the fact that this news story was a reality for our family. That had seemed to be my mode of operation when things upset me; I acted as if they didn't happen. My husband and I had interviewed the Director, toured the facility and prayed before we entrusted our baby to her care. The baby had been in that setting for almost two years after we had a bad experience at another daycare. The transition was hard, I didn't want to leave my child with anyone, but a private provider in a family-like setting felt like an easier transition than a facility. How could this have happened to us!

I sat in training class trying to ignore the images in my mind of my daughter being hurt, or worse, killed. While the pain kicked at me like a baby from the inside, I kept silent, not speaking to my classmates or my instructors. I wanted to go home and hold my baby girl. The topic of our training that day was "*Taking Care of Yourself.*" I caught a glimpse of this line in the power point that struck me like a dagger and released the pain I was trying to nurture internally: "Don't blame yourself."

Don't. Blame. Yourself.

One of the instructors was speaking, I don't know what she was talking about. I remember my arm shooting up in the air and standing at attention. I thought I was going to respond to the statement but raising my hand turned on the faucet of my emotions. I closed my eyes and let the tears pour out of me. The pain was birthed and I started to sob uncontrollably in front of all of my classmates. I could hear them talking but I didn't know what they were saying. Impatient people were telling me that I had the floor and could talk. I think my coworker was rubbing my back. I spoke through sobs, "I was late for class because my daughter's school was raided by the police this morning. The director was arrested." I was still crying, "Although no children were in the building at the time of the arrest, it was assumed that they had been there when illicit activities were occurring." People were trying to encourage me, saying things like, "You couldn't have known that was going on." Someone else said, "Don't worry about it, your baby is fine."

Another person offered, "*It's not your fault.*"

My rebuttal to those responses was defensive, "How could I not have known? How could I have let my guard down so low that my daughter was put in danger? What kind of mother am I that I did not know? One of our church mothers knew her, she came highly recommended."

The instructors allowed me to leave the class so I could get myself together. My classmates had seen my vulnerable and broken. I gathered my composure in the bathroom with a long look in my own eyes. I could not have known that a fully licensed and accredited child care provider would allegedly be engaging in illicit activity while my child and other defenseless children were present. The child care provider's intentions and actions were opposite of what I expected. She lied to us and she kept her word at the same time. What a dichotomy!

With my husband gone for the weekend, I was left alone to process my emotions. I stayed up Friday and Saturday night sitting in her room watching her sleep. I cried when no one was around me. With all of my self-blame, I could not change what had happened. My tears did not relieve my pain. I was sad and heartbroken for no reason. With my first reaction of panic to quit my job and take care of her, I was jolted into reality. I like my job AND we have bills. To my knowledge, nothing happened to my daughter. I was worried about everything that could have happened. I conjured up possible situations and shuddered at all of them. Guilt held me hostage. For a couple of weeks I found it hard to shake the "what ifs" that danced in my mind. I was watching the news and reading the newspaper and that contributed to my panic. I condemned myself and questioned the consistent caregivers who had already proven themselves capable. I called my parents and in-laws for support, they offered what they could, but their words were not salve for my wounds. I felt alone, angry and frustrated. No one comprehended that I am her mother, the mother who was supposed to protect her.

My husband was standing like a man unshaken, staunch and full of faith. When he grew tired of my self-deprecation, the man of few words that he is said, and "God kept her." My argument for being so sensitive to the issue of my child being close to danger was that even if they love her with depth, no one can replace her parents. Again, he responded, "God kept her." As he always does, my husband told me to write what I was feeling. It took some time, but the start of my personal healing started with a letter I wrote to myself from my daughter's perspective. It was watching her resilience that taught me to remember my own. I had to give myself grace (the capacity to forgive yourself and others) during a circumstance that I could not control. I wrote what I thought she would say to me.

Mommy,
I know you love me. I know that you do your best to protect me and cover me. I see that you have trusted people to love me just as much as you do. Some of them love me unconditionally and purely, others have selfish intentions.

Don't try to wrap your mind around what occurred; you may never understand. You may not have been able to know that things would happen this way but it does not change the way I feel about you.

I am worried about you. You are withdrawing from me, hiding your face when you cry and running into seclusion when you think about what happened. It's not your fault Mommy. Let's work through this together. Let me see you when you are hurting. I will grow from watching you cope and heal. I may not remember this happened at all but when I am older, you can talk to me about how God kept me safe when I can understand what that means.

You are really strong; don't forget. Please don't blame yourself. God had me in his hands and He protects me. Remember how we pray every day, God hears your prayers. Trust that you have taught me right from wrong and that even if I make a bad choice, I will recover from it. God will not depart from me. All things are working together for my good. Believe in yourself and your ability to make decisions on my behalf. Yes, I am affected by what happened, and I may have been changed, but this did not break me. Don't let it break you.

I love you Mommy,
Lovey

There are two lessons I learned through this experience. I believe that God keeps His promises to us. If you are experiencing a rough season, consider this:

1. *My prayers for protection from dangers seen and unseen had been answered.* Something instinctively led me to pray every day for a few months prior to the daycare closing. I would never let the baby leave my sight in the morning without covering her in prayer. I had been consistent for only a few months but God heard me. I now know that God keeps all of us in the palm of His hand. That is what it means to be Unpluckable.

2. *You are protected.* As I had trusted people to protect my child when she was in their care, I also trust God with my innermost desires. I believe that God keeps our assignments hidden until the season of His plan to accomplishment. He protects them when we are unable to do so.

You may make choices that put your goals at risk such as poor financial decisions, bad relationships or self-abusive behaviors, yet you still maintain your purpose. You are Unpluckable even when you do not remember your why. You can find purpose in your pain, keep walking, you are not alone.

Tending the Roots of Unpluckable Faith

Do you believe that God keeps His promises to you?

Blossoms:
Accountability In the Unpluckable
Faith Community

Re-Energize At a Retreat

The concept of people forming groups of like-minded individuals is not new. Napoleon Hill talked about "mastermind groups," Keith Ferrazi calls them "a personal board of directors." There are sororities, book clubs, professional leadership organizations and even church groups that you can get connected to if you desire to be part of this type of community.. Take an inventory of your current connections with people, are they already an Unpluckable Faith Community? One definition of the word accountability is "subject to the responsibility to report." Are the people in your life walking with you, praying for you or standing with you when you need them? Expect that this group of people (or individual) has your best interest at heart and that they agree with you about your tangible gifts.

In 2014, for my 40th birthday I planned the first "Unpluckable Retreat" at a conference center in a rural part of Pennsylvania. I invited a few of my friends to join me. I wanted to invite a small group of women and people who had read *Girl, Pray for Me*. The idea was to create time and space for them to fellowship, rest and actualize in their God-given purpose. The women prayed together, created action steps and kept in touch to monitor deadlines. Speakers were given topics to address that ranged from writing, identity and clutter, to business development, community involvement and internal barriers. The participants reported that they left the weekend full of anticipation to fulfill God's purpose for their lives. Shared, that they felt re-energzied having immersed themselves in an Unpluckable Faith Community.

The next year, I invited my spiritual mother, DeLisa to give a workshop on self care. There were tools for spiritual warfare such as plastic helmets, shields and breastplates, butterflies, tissues and mirrors. The interesting thing, is that Mama DeLisa did not know many of the women by name. When she gave a gift, she was listening to instructions from the Holy Spirit. Women in the room heard from God through her about their personal circumstances, their families and their goals. Her instructions were to use whatever object she gave them as a reminder to keep walking with God.

Before the night was over she walked over to me, looked me in the eye and said in front of everyone in the room, "Penda, what God has for you is for you but you only have enough faith for the step you are on." I started to cry because her words had confirmed my silent prayers. God had allowed me to bring all of these women together so that He could speak to them, but He had not overlooked me! God had heard me and it was my time to hear from Him.

Mama DeLisa gave the instructions "Turn the lights off." The room was dark and I was still seated. "Give me a candle." She handed me the candle and said, "You have enough faith for the step you are on.

Now you need to walk." I stood up to take a few steps and she gave more instructions: "Joi," she motioned for my friend to come to my side, "grab her arm and walk with her." I heard Mama DeLisa say, "Keep walking. You have enough faith for the step you are on. Take your steps."

While holding my arm Joi whispered in my ear, "Tell the women to walk with you." We walked around the circle and I looked everyone in the eye through my tears. I spoke their name and said, "Walk with me."

At one point I looked back at the women and they were locked in arms with one another. Many of us were in tears. I could see how some were clutched tighter than others while walking. It appeared to me that everyone was supporting someone else during the walk. The image was sealed in my mind: there are times in our lives when we will need someone to walk with us through difficult times. We may need to lean on them while they hold us up, we may need to know that they are there so we can keep walking. That moment was a visual representation of the scripture in *Ecclesiastes 4: 9-12 (KJV)* which reads:

Two are better than one, Because they have a good reward for their labor. 10 For if they fall, one ill lift up his companion. But woe to him who is alone when he falls, For he has no one to help him up. 11 Again, if two lie down together, they will keep warm; But how can one be warm alone? 12 Though one may be overpowered by another, two can withstand him. And a threefold cord is not quickly broken. (KJV)

After the weekend had concluded, the women began to share their lives with one another via e-mails and social media posts. They talked openly about programs they developed, books, job offers and hopes for their families. This Unpluckable Faith Community. group also exchanged stories of job losses, illnesses, financial difficulties, health crises and deaths of loved ones. It was interesting to hear some of them give explanations for long periods of silence. I learned from this group that shame prevented people from being honest about their progress. One admitted, *"I didn't do what I said I was going to do and I feel that I let you all down."* Because they have developed this support system, no one gets left behind. Any indication of wavering, slipping back into old habits (or ashes) is called out and corrected. People in the group may feel like they are getting drenched with rain but someone is always nearby with an umbrella and enough faith to cover them.

We illustrated what it means to be Unpluckable by using an umbrella. If you do not carry an umbrella during a rain storm it is obvious that you will get wet. When you step out of God's will you will have consequences for your disobedience. If you walk under your umbrella (of Unpluckable faith) at all times, your walk will be much easier. It is like being caught in a rain storm and having someone walk with you because their umbrella is big enough for the both of you.

Many people get their girlfriends together for getaway trips or even "night out" adventures. Whatever you need to do to build and maintain your Unpluckable Faith Community, do it and feel no shame for taking time to retreat. In these efforts you are going "home."

Who is in your Unpluckable Faith Community?

Stand Through Her Pain

What do you do when someone you love is sitting in a cave, hiding from you because they are discouraged and no longer want to walk toward their goals? How to you fall in line with their rhythm or get them to start walking. One way is to remember that there is purpose in pain. Your words can speak life or death to a person's situation, but when you don't have the words to say, just be there until they can walk again. The Bible teaches about love in II Corinthians chapter 13, in order to stand with someone as their accountability partner you have to first love them and second, agree with them in faith.

On December 6, 2011 a woman I had recently come to know took a cocktail of her own medication in an attempt to end her life. The news of KJ's hospitalization hurt me deeply. Questions plagued my mind about KJ and I was not entirely sure I had made myself available to her when things were difficult. I wondered if I had really walked with her or watched KJ walk and fall:

Did I speak to her when I saw her last?
Was I really listening when she was talking to me?
Why didn't she talk to me about this decision before . . .?
Are there others in my circle thinking about suicide?

This situation led me to recount the number of suicides of people I had heard about or, knew of personally. I attended a funeral for a woman of my church. A sixth grader I worked with at the Boys and Girls Club took his life. My aunt and a few friends had made suicide attempts. Despite all these events, I realized we don't talk about mental health or suicide prevention enough.

I remembered how our interactions, although limited, had been heartfelt. I thought KJ and I were building a strong relationship - strong enough that if she needed me, she would call me. I was greatly penetrated in my heart when I heard the news of her hospitalization. I wanted to try and do something to help her find a glimpse of hope in the darkness. It was my feeble attempt to be supportive when I was trying to understand her pain and mine. I didn't want KJ or anyone to die with unfinished business for God. I wanted to find a way to help KJ and other people in my life hear from God about their purpose---so that it might give them a reason to hold on to life.

Like Dianna Green, KJ was overwhelmed with life's circumstances when she made her suicide attempt. My husband went to see her in my stead and I recorded my thoughts in my journal. I wanted to develop an arsenal of Biblical and positive responses in case I needed to counteract any negative thoughts from KJ. I wanted to give KJ a reminder to live. Watching KJ find the strength to live after an attempt to end her life I saw as she changed her environment, let go of friends, created a structured schedule and spent time in prayer and worship.

From my immediate family to my church and work connections there were several people struggling to hear from God for an answer about their purpose. I felt the weight of their burdens on my back as I thought about KJ. Because of KJ, I began to ponder the fact that many people in my circle could no longer verbalize their aspirations with passion. Looking at friends and family it seemed like no one was living with total joy. I felt like I was always running from zombies like I see people do in movies. Everywhere I turned there was someone clawing at me saying, "I don't have dreams anymore." I was hearing people express frustration with failed attempts at goals and the fire I had seen in many people was gone.

In the magazine article "Death of a Superwoman" (Essence Magazine, March 1998), Diane Weathers chronicled the untimely death of Dianne Green, who had a lot of successes in her life and was a community activist. Her loving family and solid faith kept her grounded, yet she ended her life. Unfortunately, she had a seemingly jaded coworker who dug into her past and uncovered untruths about her educational background. As a result, Ms. Green lost her job. The collision of her failing physical health due to diabetes, losing beloved family members, and the embarrassment of publicly losing her job was too much to carry.

The boundaries that KJ created for herself were to create a safe space to heal. She through this personal detoxification helped me to recognize where my personal boundaries are lacking in my business and personal life. I pondered on the work I do for writers and how giving away free services causes a lot of stress for my family and for me. My business at that time was becoming more of a burden than a blessing to us. While giving my services away, no one could recognize the value of my work. I said to myself, "*The act of doing something that seems contrary to my own best interests is one definition of suicide.*" Wow! I had not intended to harm myself, but I was engaging in harmful behaviors. Ignoring my passion to help people be their best self in God's eyes was transforming me into a person with no creativity or zeal. I was prostituting my business to maintain friendships, giving away my services at the cost of not spending time with my family. It took KJ's suicide attempt to help me digest the fact that my hopes were dying while I was helping everyone else live theirs and as a result: my business was on life support.

In my quest to learn things about KJ, it came to light that she loves to read and edit. I created a challenge for us, "I am going to write a book in thirty days and you are going to edit it for me."
She was excited, "Let's do it!" In March of 2012, I embarked on a journey to write a book that would confront excuses that hold people back from achieving their goals. Every day I wrote a chapter and e-mailed it to her. KJ responded with constructive criticism and pushed me to write on a deeper level. While focusing on my book, I noticed that my business was also growing; people were seeking me out to edit their books for them and they were willing to pay. What a change !

After thirty days, not only did we have a finished book, but also we had invited a group of friends to join us for a discussion over breakfast. That meeting became our first Unpluckable Faith Community. For me to write and KJ to edit brought forth a book that has reached many women. That breakfast meeting was the launching of something great in us.

KJ and I were learning to walk in our gifts but we identified our excuses, recognized when we got discouraged, and found intentional tenacity to complete our God-given assignment. With this support system we are fighting to become the woman we believe in - the woman God created all of us to be. Girl, walk with me is more than a cliché, it is our lifestyle.

"Being Unpluckable means knowing that despite everything I am facing in life, I am rooted and grounded in the love and sovereignty of God. --- KJ

My connection with KJ reminded me that we all have an ability to influence a person's confidence with how we respond to them in crisis. In my quest to remind KJ of her value, I started to walk in the knowledge of my own gifts and talents. This experience helped me to get ready for my next level of ministry. As KJ and I worked together on our own personal development, the atmosphere around us started to shift; we started to act and think differently. I thank God not only for sparing KJ, but also for using her to help me recognize that I have much more living to do. I had been given a second chance.

Another one of my friends had a suicide attempt that shocked me when I heard the news. Danielle is a gifted woman with witty and creative ideas who has a diagnosis of depression. Some situations in her life have caused her to question her life and call to the ministry. At one point, she hit a wall in her search for a breakthrough and lamented to me *"I am so frustrated. I don't know what I am supposed to be doing anymore."*

What can you say to someone who feels this way? The only thing I could say was *"You are Unpluckable. Nothing can pluck you from God's hand."*

At times Danielle's depression has paralyzed her to the point where it was difficult to get out of her bed. She has described this feeling to me as a "darkness that covers my eyes." We have discussed how well-meaning people (church friends) have tried to encourage her when she feels depressed. In their eyes support is telling her to pray more or seek God to help her as if to say she is not "Christian enough" when she has this experience. Danielle revealed to me that these words have been painful and had at one point caused her to go deeper into her cave. "I don't choose to live in this darkness. There is not always something I can do to make it go away." For Suicide Prevention month, this is what Daneille shared with her friend about her struggle with depression.

September is National Suicide Prevention and Awareness Month. This is a very important issue to me. I recently got a tattoo which incorporates the semicolon symbol and the words "Hold On" with a cross. Some might ask and wonder why. In March of 2011 I attempted to take my own life. I had been battling a severe bought of depression and I had become increasingly suicidal. That Sunday morning as I began taking the bottle of pills I had planned to use to end my life a friend sent me a message that said "God told me to tell you to Hold On!" She went on to say that she was not sure why she was sending me that message but felt it was urgent. Little did she know at the time those words literally saved my life. I had already taken several pills and I had the rest in my hand to swallow. I put them down and cried for hours. It was then that I was able to start the slow and painful process of telling my mother and trying to get help. This tattoo is a reminder to me to hold on to life and that my life's story is not over yet (that's what the semicolon is for).

I thank God that He sent folks my way to help me fight for life when I believed I no longer had a reason to live. Always encourage someone who may be suicidal to seek help! Suicide prevention and awareness is crucial. You could save a life! But not if you don't know the warning signs or the steps to take to help. You should NEVER guilt or blame someone who has lost all hope and is feeling like they don't have a reason to live.

I was the friend who sent Danielle that text message and we were in two different states. As part of an Unpluckable Faith Community I encourage you to be obedient when you are instructed by the Holy Spirit to reach out to someone. I was walking with Danielle and did not know what she needed! God has proven to me on several occasions that my obedience was necessary. Your obedience is necessary as are your gifts and talents were given to you by God. Nothing can separate you from the love of God *(Romans 8:28 KJV)*. As the Semicolon Project says on its website, *"Your story is not over yet."* Remind people in your Unpluckable Faith community that their promise, purpose and position is in God's hand.

Tending the Roots of Unpluckable Faith

Do you remember that your promise, purpose and position is in God's hand?

Don't Give Up On Her

One of my closest friends has not been able to recognize or embrace her purpose since we were awkward girls with braces and braids. Robin is in her forties and does not believe that she has had a fulfilling life; this mentality has debilitated her. It is hard to get her to understand that she has a purpose and is necessary in the kingdom of God. So many things have happened which have caused Robin to fight for her life, literally. For most of the time I have known her, Robin has stood in the middle of an invisible boxing ring with low self-esteem as her opponent taunting, *"Stand up! Fight back!"*

Throughout our friendship of over thirty years we have mapped our goals together. From party dresses to clothes for our babies, we have celebrated our achievements. Robin has always wanted more for her life that what she has accomplished and unfortunately has been unable to grasp what she desires. Her inability to fight the invisible enemy of low self-esteem is the result of experiences, which she thought deflated her value over time. My friendship with Robin has taught me about relentless fervor. Robin has a lot of what I call "Spike stories." Although setbacks paralyzed her courage to pursue goals it did not affect her mental capacity, Robin never quits. I have witnessed her fight until the end even when her shadow in the boxing ring is looming with an inevitable victory.

"Spike stories" are traumatic and challenging situations, which can happen to anyone. The term "Spike stories" came from watching my beloved Shih Tzu puppy get mauled by a neighbor's two pit bulls. The neighbor's dogs did not let go of Spike until their goal was complete – they were being trained to fight. I was devastated in that rite of passage moment and losing Spike Lee Doggy under those traumatic circumstances taught me some hard lessons about goals. My puppy ran through my legs to face off against larger and stronger dogs because he had a responsibility to protect me. I was the intended target! To understand that my dog was intentional to fulfill his goal of protecting me liberated me from the guilt I was carrying about losing him.

In retrospect of my "Spike story," I want people to pursue their goals with the same fervor as all three dogs. If we want it, we cannot let go until either God says no, or we achieve it. Robin reminds me of the pit-bulls I have seen her consistently try to lock on her goals. Her inability to accomplish goals is often due to circumstances beyond her control. No matter how many times Robin has failed in attempt to pursue her goals, she never has quit anything - she plants her feet and fights for her life even when she has been forced to stop pursuing a goal (due to bad credit, a background check, etc.). One of Robin's biggest goals was to become a nurse. When she went to nursing school she did not pass the introductory courses required and had to withdraw. I have shuddered when she got hit with lies that destroyed her character, career choices that caused her to question herself, and bad decisions that have ripped apart her credit score. Her background check, her bank account, her education – you name it, there is always something preventing her from achieving some of her goals. Like many of us, Robin has internalized her letdowns and has had to remove the label she put on herself: Failure.

For most of her goals Robin has (in her own eyes) always fallen short; she cannot seem to get past former mistakes and neither can some of the people around her. Each choice she makes reminds her of a decision she made in the past---and that reminds her of a dream she had---which reminds her of...

Do you get the picture? It has been an endless cycle that she cannot seem to break. Robin has the strength to keep trying, even when no one believes that she should. Robin does not always give herself permission to forgive herself for her failures or the courage to move beyond a setback. Getting focused on these situations is what keeps her stuck in circumstances that she despises. Because of her letdowns, Robin has not found a stable place to erect her self-worth. She is wedged between her goals and achievement because she has heard the word "No" so many times that she does not recognize opportunities when they are authentic. She is learning to recognize when things are coming to steal, kill and destroy her faith. *(John 10:8-10, KJV)*

Robin's greatest battle has been recognizing her significance and identifying the things she has done well. When she forgets that she is an amazing mother, a devoted sister, worthy of being respected, I put on my boxing gloves and fight for her. Oddly, I am often fighting Robin. She has for years isolated herself in the boxing ring with her two opponents: the woman she wants to become and the woman who has believed the labels placed on her. From the outside the fighting appears senseless but for Robin, the fight is a necessary part of her existence. Fighting is all she knows after all of these years of feeling unworthy.

"Not every failure is bad." I tell her. *"Some failures are not failures. "*

"I feel stuck." This response is difficult to counteract. I want her to know that she is Unpluckable, which is stuck, but not in the way she describes. I know that there is greatness buried under Robin's pain. When she wants to quit and feels defeated I do not allow her to wallow in self-pity. I have heard every one of her reasons for being stuck: struggles with being a single mother, bad boyfriends, loved ones dying, homelessness, and dead-end jobs. These circumstances remind her that she has made mistakes; they remind me of her resilience and strength. Look at the irony there! Sometimes perspective is all that we need. I want Robin to make her invisible hurts visible to someone in order to get healing. In an attempt to shatter the sound proof walls she has built around herself I think it is imperative to tell her the truth even when it hurts me to speak the words and when it hurts her to hear them. This has meant at times that I have had to raise my voice and yell at her so that my words resonate through those barriers. This is what we do for each other as friends, we uplift one another as much as possible. I tell Robin, "Your problem has never been your past; the problem has always been how you think about your future." I cannot be with Robin all the time, at some point she has to learn to lean on her own faith in God as do we all. *How many people do you know like Robin? Are you like Robin?*

Several years ago Robin made a great sacrifice in search of her purpose. By donating her kidney to her sister she gained a new perspective about what is important to her. Having known of her sister's condition since she was eleven years old she always felt helpless to help her until the time was right and she was old enough to handle the responsibility of being a donor. Robin spoke about how the surgery gave her a renewed sense of determination to accomplish something significant in her life:

Before the surgery, I felt like a lost soul. My life was unstable in relationships, employment and within my family. I wore a mask to try to fit in everywhere I went, but I was living in a hole of depression. When I recovered from the surgery, not only did I realize that God had chosen me to help save my sister's life but my eyes were opened to the possibilities that I could be more, and do more with my life. I finally felt that my life had meaning. My family seemed to be disappointed with me and constantly upset about my poor choices, but in their eyes I became visible again after I gave my sister my kidney. Giving my sister my kidney gave us both a second chance at life.

Robin was recently hospitalized for a week. Her doctors could not figure out what was ailing her, a virus was shutting her body down. She did not tell me immediately that she was sick; we had made plans to travel together and the doctor did not approve her release from the hospital. When I found out that she was in the hospital I was distraught. I reflected on the unfinished goals she has yet to accomplish. I asked myself, Will Robin ever get to experience total joy?

Some failures, are not failures.

Although it has been a process Robin has wrestled with herself to proclaim that she is necessary. Robin has been knocked down but she bounces back after every challenge. When you are standing on the outside of a boxing ring watching your goal setter crawl around the bottom of the boxing ring – call out to them so they can stand again. The longer they lie down, the more they will listen to the lies swirling above them. Remind them that part of learning to walk is falling down but standing up builds muscles and strength. With every elevation they are closer to their transformation. Tell them your story of being in that boxing ring. When they hear how you overcame through your faith, they may have the strength to walk again.

Tending the Roots of Unpluckable Faith

What is your "Spike Story?"

Girl, Walk With Me | Unpluckable Faith and Accountability

Evaluate Your Preconceptions

I did not understand until Maya Angelou died that there can be conditions beyond a person's control that influence how they approach their goals. Some people cannot go back to get things they sacrificed due to sickness, divorce; (you can list others reasons _____). I now understand how important it is to grieve the loss of your dream after a setback. In time, healing and a new perspective do come and we as an Unpluckable Faith community have to give *Goal Seekers* time to recognize barriers and teach them how to overcome them.

My experience with the death of Maya Angelou forced me to change how I treated people with unfulfilled goals. *"Penda, I don't have dreams."*

There was a time that whenever someone made the above statement I would laugh in disbelief. I was questioning the validity of the sentiment and at the same time trying to tackle the idea that a person could live a full life without a gift, or goal stirring inside of them. Often I would hear, "I don't know what I want to do with my life." I cannot tell you if I inherited the paradigm dreams are what a person lives for from my own experiences, from my family or if I created the belief system on my own.

This statement sounded to me like the person was espousing a lack of ambition. In reality, many of those people were embracing the raw and painful reality of setbacks in their life. They had attempted to accomplish a goal and for whatever reason, did not accomplish it. How could they, in that moment, define and create a plan to pursue a goal when failure was looming over them? After an injury a person has to take time to heal, if they do not, they could cause more harm to themselves. As we know, some wounds are life changing; we see that with accidents that create brain or spine injuries. After a loss or a failure, life may not always go back to "the normal reality."

When my friend Jaki was living in a shelter she shared her frustrations with me about having to give up her life the way she knew it to move into a shelter. Her focus was on her present moment, gaining everything she needed from the experience so she could walk into a life after the shelter without the brokenness that she carried with her. Jaki created a plan to live day-to-day so that as she planned for her future, she would remember her life when it was broken. Jaki intentionally put her personal goals on hold so she could heal spiritually and emotionally. Others seem to exist in the moment of pain – living in their failure without recognizing that through pain healing comes and growth is a process.

During the time in my life when I could not comprehend how a person could be displeased with their life and not change it I was hypercritical. When I have heard people express that there is no better way, "This is just how my life is," or "This is just my fate." I would become incensed at them. I felt like they were complaining and making excuses instead of creating change. I think because my belief system became distorted over the years I began to push people too hard to run after a dream or a goal before it was their season.

Finally I understand that there is a difference between a choice to do nothing and a barrier preventing a person from moving forward. We do not always have to push so hard to accomplish a goal, appreciating the process is an important and necessary part of our growth. Thoughtfulness is more important than speed. I think Caren Baginski summed up the process of dreaming and going after your goals beautifully when she penned on her blog, "Lack of motivation or action toward completing your dream doesn't mean it's not real or that you don't want it. It's that you haven't figured out how to turn the wanting into doing. And maybe you haven't figured out what it is that you really, really want." The article is entitled, "Five Ways to Motivate Yourself to Live Your Dream. " This author helped re-frame my paradigm about how to respond when people cannot verbalize their aspirations.

I wanted to meet the writer, speaker and teacher Maya Angelou since I was fourteen years old. I Know Why the Caged Bird Sings was required reading in my eighth grade Honors English class. During that time, as all adolescents I was searching for my identity. The introduction to Maya Angelou and her poem "Phenomenal Woman" inspired me to look at myself differently. Bullying at school and in the neighborhood had led me to internalize that I did not deserve to be a beautiful, smart, happy or valuable human being. Maya Angelou had written about some of the same things I was experiencing and her writing was the catalyst for me to tell my story.

It became a dream to thank Maya Angelou personally for pouring water on me with her words. I often dreamed of the day I would meet my hero and what I would say when I was able to make a human connection. I recall hearing Maya Angelou speak once but I was in a large auditorium and did not have a chance to shake her hand. As an adult I wanted to meet her, to thank her for writing and figuratively bow down in the presence of greatness. I thought that meeting Maya Angelou was a non-negotiable ambition but I did not put forth the work to make it happen. If it were a priority I would have worked hard for it like I did when as a student in college. Until I put in the work to prove that my goals are priorities in my life, they will not happen. Obviously I made my desire to meet Maya Angelou a desire until the option to meet her was no long available to me.

On the day that Maya Angelou died I received several phone calls from friends and family members. I was in my cubicle wearing my ear buds when my coworker yelled over the cubicle "Penda are you okay?"
"Yeah. Why?"
"Maya Angelou just died. I saw it come across CNN."

I took a deep breath to hold back my tears and walked as quickly as I could to the elevator. I bit my tongue to keep the emotions intact but when I got outside I bowed over in tears. I did not care who was watching me or who was walking past the courtyard, I allowed myself to cry as I sat on the cold concrete steps. When I felt calm enough I called my friend Sheri.

Sheri answered the phone. "Are you OK?"

I couldn't respond immediately. "I never got to meet her." I spoke through my tears, which had welled up again.

"I know Penda. I know." Nan-C and Sheri were already preparing themselves to help me through the loss. "Nan was just watching the news to confirm it was true before we called you."

"My coworker just told me. I was not on news sites today at work."
"What are you going to do now?" Sheri's voice helped me calm down.
"I don't know." Tears were still falling and my head was starting to hurt. Sheri was strong, "I will tell you what you are going to do. You are going to keep writing. You will carry on her legacy."

I rolled my eyes at that statement. "I won't be writing for a while Sheri."

"You will write." That was a stern response that made me stand at attention just like Jaki had when she told me to listen. "You have to keep writing Penda, you might be the world's next Maya Angelou. Even if you're not, you have to keep writing."

I thanked Sheri for her support and ended our call. What she said about me, "... the next Maya Angelou," meant that she saw greatness in me through my gifts and talents as a writer. We agreed that I cannot compare to Maya Angelou but I could pick up the torch of being a Scribe for our generation.

For the next few weeks I answered inquiries from friends and family about how I was going to move forward in with my aspirations since Maya Angelou had died. "Dreams are for the birds," was my only response. I said this so cliché so much that my husband RJ suggested I research the origin of the cliché. *"You need to understand where that phrase came from, your desire to meet Maya Angelou was real. It can't be erased with a cliché."* So I took his advice.

The cliche *"For the birds."* originated in the 1800's when horses were the country's main source of transportation. People were accustomed to seeing horse dung and the common language became, *"That s--- is for the birds!"* Birds, clueless to the fact that dung is unsanitary were gathering nourishment from manure. This understanding of birds led me to wonder what I am willing to do to get to my life sustaining goals.

At times I have chosen to do both, dig through the dung of my past, the weeds of my rejection and fight for what I believe God has given my hands to do. When I have dug through these things I have recognized the dung and sifted through it to get the wisdom I needed. Other times I have turned my nose up at the thought of dung and walked away from it, choosing bless the birds. With my dream to meet Maya Angelou, I chose to leave it but the internal fight forced me to find what I needed and shift my position. This is what I want you to do, dig through the negative comments, the rejection and fear you feel so you can get to your dream!

A few weeks after Maya Angelou's funeral (which I watched online) I reflected on a conversation my husband and I had after seeing the movie *The Pursuit of Happyness*. I was inspired after seeing this movie with him in 2006. He jokes that I never allow him to watch anything in peace because I lean over and interrogate him while he is trying to relax. During this movie I was in his ear the whole time. One part of the film that resonated with me is when Christopher Gardner and his son had to lock themselves in the subway bathroom to sleep because they were homeless. People were banging on the door and Mr. Gardner was holding his son in his arms rocking him and crying. I think I was crying too. I did not have a child at the time but when I look at my daughter I know how it feels to sacrifice for her.

In *The Pursuit of Happyness*, Will Smith ran in almost every scene of the movie. This demonstrated to me how Chris Gardner literally had to run after his dream. He was running to catch the bus. He ran to catch thieves. He was running to pick up the baby on time from daycare because he could not afford late fees. I wanted to find something I could run after too and I remember asking my husband when the movie ended, "What dream do you have that you would run for?" RJ's response infuriated me, "I don't have dreams." I left him in the movie theater and walked to the car.

Words for a Dandelion: Thank you Maya Angelou

On bad days my friend "Dano" whispered words –
Your words that rebuked, inspired and encouraged me:
"Pretty women wonder. . ."

Like a thirsty flower tasting water for the first time
My spirit stood at attention and my confidence was arrested.
Each time I heard your words recited, courage and hope enveloped me;
I found myself again.
". . . where my secret lies."

Madame Angelou
You greatly impacted me; in your shadow I found strength.
Your words took root inside of 14 year old me.
I want to pour into the future, embrace the past, and keep my head up
NO MATTER WHAT!
From a distance you poured water on a droopy dandelion
when life's droughts nearly choked it.

When I feel lost, I remember my strength when I embrace the women in my circle who bring pieces of
me back home.

I see you in my Grandmothers - think of your wisdom when I sit at their feet.
I hear you in my mother, she is bound in second chances
proud, capable, and hopeful for me, her daughter, sister-friend.
I wrap my sister in my arms and hold her when she wants to fall,
Whispering "and still I rise."

I thank God.
He gave you the talent to put words together in a symphony that has played the backdrop of my life's purpose and watered it.

Thank you, thank you, and I thank you.
Penda L. James (2012)

Being part of an Unpluckable Faith Community, try to filter your perspective consistently through the word of God. You do not want to seem distant, cold or disrespectful to people in your responses to them. Until Maya Angelou died, I did not comprehend how a person in my circle could live without dreams. When she died, I became, clueless, frustrated and rehearsing my failures. I was grieving Maya Angelou's death privately and jealous while hearing from numerous people proud to share their memories of having met her. I was trying to express joy for them and confront my disappointment but the death of my dream was at the forefront. No one seemed to understand why I was grieved by the death of Maya Angelou. After numerous frustrating conversations with people who were minimizing my frustration it hit me *---this must be how people feel when I respond to them and their answer is not strong enough in my opinion.* I could not verbalize that meeting Maya Angelou was about the opportunity for me to show an author that books change lives. I have been told that my books have changed lives and I wanted to tell Maya Angelou that she was "rocking the world" with her impact.

Was I equating meeting Maya Angelou with my personal success as a writer? There is no other explanation for my distress. While living through my own dream collapse, I realized how disappointment can affect a person and their outlook on pursuing goals. The death of my dream revealed my forceful nature of pushing people without understanding their "why" in pursuing a goal. My intention behind insisting that the people connected to me would live in abundance according to God's plan for them. I did not want anyone to "die dead" as I heard Uncle Spirit say on the reality show Flex and Shanice. I can admit that I was expecting my friends and family to move forward and push a restart button after a failure without considering how disappointment, discouragement or rejection can feel when they sit on you unattended.

Let me give you an illustration of how rejection and disappointment feel when they "sit" on you. When my daughter was three years old I took her to the park so she could play. The park was large so we had a lot of walking to do in order to get from the car to the playground. She spent about an hour running back and forth from the slide to the swings and spinning on the "merry go round." When I saw she was getting tired I started toward the car. We walked a few steps before she asked, "Can you pick me up?"

It was her custom to be picked up and climb on my shoulders. She was so depleted of energy that she put her chin on my head and clenched my throat, literally choking me to prevent from falling. She was falling asleep on my shoulders and after a while of carrying her in that position, I started to get tired. I could feel the weight of her 30 pounds pulling me down. My back was bowing under the pressure and as much as I aimed to make her comfortable, I was uncomfortable. As we drew a few feet from the car, I had to put her down. When will we stop carrying the weight of rejection, disappointment and discouragement? When will we start giving our fears to God and casting our cares on Him? Much like my daughter became heavy during that walk with her on my shoulder, unfulfilled goals get heavy.

Barriers are circumstances that have potential to prevent a person from completing a task. Some people stop at the barrier while others find creative ways to break through them. An example of a person breaking through barriers is a woman I met who wanted to be a professional dancer. She trained for years as a dancer and in her late adolescent years had a health-related injury to her leg that ended her dance career. This barrier breaker puts her energy into teaching dance and raising awareness about child abuse. She found a way to be creative in staying connected to her dream even though she can no longer dance. Another example of a barrier breaker is a student in college who chose a major and could not passing a critical course or a required exam. The student either retakes the class or recognizes that they need to declare a new major.

What about people who experience rejection that seems to build brick walls in front of them when they make a decision to accomplish a goal? How do they find a way to try again after experiencing the devastation of failure? One way is to answer the hard questions that lead them to the root of the problem. Questions like "When I don't achieve the one thing I set out do to, do I just live to die?"

Some people equate being "stuck" to existing. There is no joy in anything; they live without expectation of success. It is easy for a person who has never been "stuck" to respond in this way: "You better not do that!" or "Find something deep inside your heart that gives you motivation to live with enthusiasm." Some people living with disappointment find it challenging to go back to the root of their faith. It is difficult to verbalize the "why." But I can sympathize with this person, I say, "Try again" and ask them these questions:

- *Is this one dream the only dream out there for you?*
- *Can you find something else to do?*
- *How can you recover from setbacks that knock you down continually?*
- *What is the real motivating factor for you to complete something you start?*

Does the reality of barriers give a person permission to form excuses? Absolutely not! If you measure success by tenacity then in fact, each time you set out with feverish persistence to accomplish a goal, by that measure you are already a success. Proverbs 18:21 says, "Words kill, words give life; they're either poison or fruit – you choose (MSG). I gained understanding about goal setting when talking with a colleague, Eric Smith. He told me, "Penda, turn dreams into goals." What Eric taught me is that if we create mini goals, we will be more successful at achieving them. "Some people would say dreams are only good for us when we are asleep. Goals are different. A goal is something we aim toward and put action behind. A goal has a deadline."

Now I want to encourage you to pray with and for those in your Unpluckable Faith Community. Allow your faith to steer you to places you have yet to imagine. Everyone in your community has great things to accomplish - not just one thing, great things. As a group how will you fortify the gifts stirring inside of you? Will you have the courage to point our areas where your Unpluckable Faith Community can seize opportunities that God places in your path?

Get out of what you find comfortable so that you can gain exposure to new opportunities. With Unpluckable Faith, you will have a commitment to purpose. If you still have goals, they are not for the birds! Keep walking until you get to the finish line. Your words have power.

Tending the Roots of Unpluckable Faith

What are you going to do now?

Walking Together

To close out *Girl, Walk with Me* I want to leave you with a few words of women from an *Unpluckable Faith Community* that I have formed. The participants wanted you to hear from them the value of having an Unpluckable Faith Community and what a group of people supporting them can do. You may have your own examples.

Wearing the #UnpluckableMe T-shirt

Two participants of the Unpluckable Retreat in 2015 by chance wore their "#UnpluckableMe" t-shirt on the same day. They each chose the shirt that day because they wanted to make an outward declaration about their faith. Jennifer had shared with the group that her son was having some legal challenges and had asked the group to pray for her. On this particular day she prayed specifically for God to show himself to her and here is her story:

Good evening sisters. This morning my son had another hearing. I got up this morning prayed and said to myself, I'm going to put on my tight UNPLUCKABLE shirt!!! "I need a maternity one!! LOL. I said, "Lord please send me an Angel!!" My anxiety was on high, "Lord show your face," I prayed. Well we were standing in the hall and guess who came around the corner my UNPLUCKABLE SISTER!! LaDina Anderson! Yes Lord!!! He knew I needed a UNPLUCKABLE SISTER! She stayed with us until they called us back. My son was offered a plea. It was dropped down to two charges from five. God SHOWED UP AND OUT!! Thank you Lord! Thank God for my UNPLUCKABLE SISTERS!

Maryn's Story...

Sooooo this morning I was sleep deprived, running late, couldn't figure out what to wear. My eyes landed on my Unpluckable Me shirt and I said "Yup, I gotta wear it today! Even though it's too cold for a tee." I was determined to wear my matching cowboy boots too even though they still need broken in and it took forever to get them on. Running late to work, I got there and proceeded to run around the building fixing stuff and responding to crazy. I was in office and there was a group of folks sitting at a computer. One of the girls stopped me and said, Ooh what's that on your shirt?" Another sister at work knew exactly what it was! I quickly explained, "It says Unpluckable Me, it's a book, it's a movement." Because I was rushing around and I believe myself to be in mixed company (believers and folks who may or may not be). The same girl with the question says, "What does it mean?" Again, I'm running and I said, "Well it's based in scripture, the reference is escaping me right now." The same girl says, "Oh you mean that you won't be plucked out of the Father's hand?" I'm like "YES!" The next thing you know, we started talking about Jesus and Christianity and Girl, Pray for Me and how it helps you on your walk. She was ecstatic because she knew Penda too. I would have NEVER foreseen a conversation like that with this girl. You just never know what God is working on and who you will encounter. Then to read what Jennifer Williams just posted?! Glory to God for this little old t-shirt! I was posting selfies and walking around, not even really thinking about it! Not knowing that I was standing in solidarity with our sister and her son! Sometimes I'm just flabbergasted by our Father and his Providence!

Writing a Book

Walking together means that there will be lengths of time that you will need to endure with a person until they feel confident enough to take the first step on their own. I have shared the story of my friend Peaches, but if you have never heard it, she is the inspiration for the book, *Girl, Pray for Me*. When I first met her she confessed to me that she had always wanted to write a book but did not have the time to write. The reality of her situation was not that she did not have the time, but that she did not want to feel what she needed to feel in order to write it. As part of her Unpluckable Faith Community, those of us in her Unpluckable Faith Community learned how to practice long suffering with a her. Even though Peaches, like Robin often finds herself at the bottom of a boxing ring fighting herself, she knows that when she finally sits down to write, she will free not only herself from the pain, but everyone who reads her book. Here is an example of her view of accountability:

When I met Penda, God showed me a book, my story and I was afraid to write it down. Penda checks on me and always asks if I have written anything, and of course the answer is, "Girl, Pray for me! Every time I start to write and the pain surfaces, I cry and move away from the keyboard." She pushed me to contribute to her book Free To Fly: Wisdom for the Seasons in a Woman's Life. I did it and it felt like a weight was lifted from that small piece. I know I will feel free once I start the journey but I have started over and over again never coming to a completion. Girl, Pray for Me and Girl, Walk with Me are excellent examples of why I have to finish my book, I understand the impact that words can have on people's lives if they are written down.

The Benefit of Self-Care

Diana, another member challenged the group to think about some of the things we do to take care of ourselves in the midst of our other responsibilities. This discussion caused people to challenge one another to try new things and obtain new tools for self-care. Although some of the members in the community did not create a self-care list, the question opened up great discussion for us. Here is her story: So in a different group I belong to, the creator posted what self-care is for her. Often we need to declare what it means to take care of ourselves-because it's not the same for everyone. Here is my list:

• Having a cup of tea, banana and a muffin/croissant every morning while responding to morning emails
• Yoga in the morning when I wake and at night before I sleep (haven't quite mastered this but I need to-it makes me happy and gives me time to center, be still and pray differently)
• Taking time to talk with my 16 year old even though I have to constantly yell cause he don't listen (those moments of forced talking provides moments of peace in my house)

- Tackling clutter in bites instead of trying to lock myself in until it's done
- Saying "No" even when it's easy for me to do what is being asked simply because it counters what I need in that moment
- Speaking up even when I feel like no one cares about what I'm saying because hearing myself voice it out loud is necessary
- Forcing myself to engage in social activities and meet new people, growth comes from uncomfortable situations
- Eating cake (it makes my insides smile)
- Letting people exit my life without finding a reason to make them stay

The responses from the Unpluckable Faith Community were thought-provoking and caused some of the women to jump into action so that they could be creative about finding rest to restore their Unpluckable Faith. One woman said, I" am a master at taking care of others. I can produce an entire list of those things but cannot come up with one thing I do to take care of myself." When members stated that they do not take time for themselves, they were challenged by the group to find something to do just for themselves with deadlines. Here are some of the responses:

- Washing my hair after a hard day
- Walking at lunch ALONE
- Drinking a cup of hot water with lemon
- ZUMBA!
- Talking to my elders once a week
- Odd waking hours, sitting in the bed reflectively pondering life and praying
- Worst Cooks in America, anything that makes me laugh hard out loud
- Spearmint!
- Coloring books
- A good book and a blanket
- Long and genuine hugs that clutch my soul
- Massages
- Crafts
- Consignment and thrift shopping
- Riding in my car with the sunroof open and hair blowing (love this)
- Listening to jazz while I cook or do chores
- Singing anywhere
- Drinking eggnog lattes at Christmas
- Buying VERY discounted Christmas items
- Swimming

I hope that you have a better understanding of what it means to have Unpluckable Faith. Let this book be a springboard for you to do your own research about faith, purpose, walking with Christ and accountability. Develop your own plans and confirm your purpose with your consistent and intentional prayer time. Ultimately, the only person you need to please is God. Do your work, and make this declaration, "With God, nothing is impossible!"

Here are a few points I want you to take with you about being Unpluckable:

1.) *Failure or disappointments can give you the fuel you need to find your rightful place.*

2.) *Trust yourself and trust God, your goals are significant.*

3.) *Dreams are for the birds. So fly!*

4.) *Do something other than wishing you were doing something!*

5.) *Sometimes when you are learning to walk, you will fall. Get up and try again.*

6.) *If you pay attention, God will reveal the emptiness in your heart where your goals reside.*

7.) *God is sovereign.*

8.) *Build an Unpluckable Faith Community, find a mentor and an accountability partner to help you achieve your goals.*

9.) *Timelines on goals prevent you from wasting time pouting about failures.*

10.) *I am feelin' fine, satisfied, and happy.*

11.) *You may not say, "Girl, Walk with me," but there will be a time when you will need to ask for help with something. Remember, Jesus had help to do His work also. He sent the disciples out in pairs. You don't have to walk alone. Build your Unpluckable Faith and Accountability.*

Did you forget that learning to walk is a process? What are some of your self-care affirmations?

Sowing an Unpluckable Garden: Exercises

lang
living with
where I turned
people express from

In th

There has been space throughout this book for you as an individual to engage with the topics we discussed through questions and activities. Asking yourself and your Unpluckable Faith Community hard questions will assist you in being specific, intentional and focused about doing God's work. Having a goal is one thing but doing the work necessary to accomplish your goals is putting action behind your faith. In the next few pages, give yourself permission to let go of what you no longer want and embrace what you need to move forward. You can do these activities individually or in small groups. Use the journal space to doodle, draw, write and pour out what you think about as it comes to you. This is a safe space for you to be yourself. I am warning you, be prepared to emerge from this process with renewed vision.

As you read Girl, Walk with Me you heard from many people who shared their interpretation of what it means to be Unpluckable. You read about their victories through challenges that have illustrated the power of God in their lives. May their "I" stories strengthen your faith. This is the power of second chances. We all now dare to find your true purpose. Here is a prayer to help you get started:

> *Lord your Word says that you will give us witty inventions. I pray that you open my eyes that I may see your glory, even if all I see is the hand of the enemy approaching me. I commit my vision to you, I ask that you renew my perception so that I may continue to serve you with my vision. Remove fear and doubt from my vocabulary. In Jesus' name. Amen.*

Girl, Walk With Me

Describe your feelings while watching someone stumble. Does it make you angry, frustrated or disappointed? Why did you feel that way?

How did they express their confusion and what do you believe they needed to begin walking toward their goals?

Girl, Walk With Me

Think about someone in your life who has made the same mistakes continuously. How did you support them in making a change?

Have you been paralyzed by a circumstance which prevented you from moving forward on one of your goals? What happened?

Rock the World

Make a list of some things you want to accomplish in your life.

Rock the World

Use the space below to record a portion of your testimony. When you feel comfortable share it with someone. Start it with, *"I Am Changed. . ."*

Rock the World

Choose something you are pursuing right now and write your *"why statement"* with your reasons to pursue that goal. When you feel discouraged and want to stop walking, this "why statement" can become a road map and a reminder not to quit walking.

The Heart of Amani

When you were required to put a goal to rest, what characteristics did you learn about yourself that you can apply to future goal pursuits?

Why were you pursuing that goal in the first place?

The Heart of Amani

Was it your wish to fulfill that goal or was it in God's purposes for you?

How did having to lay it to rest affect you?

Where Are You?

Make a list of hobbies and activities that you may have wanted to achieve "once upon a time"? Have you accomplished any of them?

Where Are You?

How do you choose your activities and responsibilities? Do you think you are letting people down if you choose to discontinue some of your obligations?

Where Are You?

How can you recover from setbacks that knock you down continually?

Go Home

Describe what it would mean for you to be feelin' fine, satisfied and happy.

Go Home

If you are, or have been a mentor, what qualities do you try to impart into your mentee?

Go Home

Who are the people in your life that help you feel at "home?"

See the Vision

Take some time to write your own definition of what it means to be Unpluckable. How can you apply it to walking in the path of God's purpose for your life?

Stand Through Her Pain

Write a poem using a color and a smell to describe what liberty feels like so that you can share that with someone in your Unpluckable Faith Community.

My Color Poem:
I walked through red to the other side of my existence
Drawn by the sweet smell of honeysuckle
I followed His hand until there was no looking back.
Dripping with His love I help others find their way home.
I stumble but the sweet fragrance of liberty stands me on my feet.
Unpluckable Me.

Stand Through Her Pain

Make a list of things in your life that are worth fighting for:

Stand Through Her Pain

Ask five people what you contribute to their lives and record their responses:

God Keeps His Promises

Write about a time when God kept His promises to you:

Be Daring

Write your thoughts about every goal you can verbalize until you empty out. Consider inviting a few friends over to have a vision board party. This will also help you see what you have written.

Be Daring

Write your thoughts about every goal you can verbalize until you empty out. Consider inviting a few friends over to have a vision board party. This will also help you see what you have written.

Unpluckable Cards

USING THE UNPLUCKABLE CARDS

Habakkuk 2:2 instructs us to *"write the vision and make it plain. . ."* The cutouts on the next few pages are designed for you to personalize your goals and *Unpluckable* declarations. Write scriptures, affirmations and prayers to post on your vision board, place in your daily planner or, to put on your mirror. Post these cutouts in visible places. I encourage you to write your vision so that you can walk it out. There are duplicates of the cutouts for you to share a few with others in your Unpluckable Faith community. Be creative, use color and be specific.

Walking In Unpluckable Faith: Affirmations

1.) Failure or disappointments can give you fuel to find your rightful place.
2.) Trust yourself and trust God. Your vision is holy. Your goals are significant.
3.) Dreams are for the birds. So fly!
4.) Do something other than wishing you were doing something!
5.) Get up and try again.
6.) God will reveal the emptiness in your heart where your goals reside.
7.) God is sovereign.
8.) Find a mentor and an accountability partner to help you achieve your goals.
9.) Timelines on goals prevent you from wasting time pouting about failures.
10.) I am feelin' fine, satisfied, and happy.

-------------------- *Cut along this line. Need More? Photocopy this page.* --------------------

#Unpluckable Defined

Unpluckable means not being easily derailed by challenges

Example:
"My friend was unpluckable through the death of her mother."

#Unpluckable Defined

A person's mentality of resilience that allows them to stay focused

Example:
"Penda is unpluckable."

---------------------- Cut along this line. Need More? Photocopy this page. ----------------

#Unpluckable Defined

Having a firm foundation of spiritual and mental faith.

Example:
"I am unpluckable like a dandelion. My roots are strong and I will bounce back."

MY UNPLUCKABLE GOALS

----------------- Cut along this line. Need More? Photocopy this page. -----------------

MY UNPLUCKABLE GOALS

MY UNPLUCKABLE GOALS

---------------- Cut along this line. Need More? Photocopy this page. ----------------

MY UNPLUCKABLE GOALS

MY UNPLUCKABLE GOALS

---------------- Cut along this line. Need More? Photocopy this page. ----------------

MY UNPLUCKABLE GOALS

My Unpluckable Declaration

---------------- Cut along this line. Need More? Photocopy this page. ----------------

My Unpluckable Declaration

My Unpluckable Declaration

----------------- *Cut along this line. Need More? Photocopy this page.* -----------------

My Unpluckable Declaration

My Unpluckable Declaration

---------------- *Cut along this line. Need More? Photocopy this page.* ----------------

My Unpluckable Declaration

Share Your Unpluckable Story!

There is opportunity for you to connect with me and other readers of Girl, Walk With Me. You can share your experience via e-mail at inscribedinspiration@gmail.com, on Twitter @Penscribed or, on Facebook using the address below.

Join the Girl, Walk With Me Community

The *Girl, Walk with Me* community is an interactive group designed to foster community and account-ability for people who have read **Girl, Pray for Me** and **Girl, Walk with Me.** By joining the group, you can:

- Connect with other readers who are actively pursuing their goals
- Network with business owners, artists, and other Goal Seekers
- Participate in an online Unpluckable Faith community
- Be an inspiration to a Goal Seeker who has stopped walking

Join the group at: https://www.facebook.com/groups/GirlWalkwithMe/

Want to do more? Reach out to discuss opportunities to:

- Host a reading group for Girl, Walk with Me
- Sponsor a retreat
- Speak to a group of people and share your "I story"

More Inspirations from InSCRIBEd Inspiration

Order Today at: http://www.unpluckablefaith.com

Girl, Pray for Me | Penda L. James | $10 + Shipping

Everyone has dreams, not everyone has intentional tenacity. Girl, Pray for Me will help you shatter excuses, overcome procrastination and confront fears. You already know how to accomplish goals; the guided journal exercises will help you define what you need in an accountability partner and think intentionally about your action steps.

Water Ain't Blue Enough | Claudia Mason | $12.99 + Shipping

Cherelle Roberts is a troubled soul who is unable to cope with the rejection of those whom she dearly loves. This rejection causes her to escape to places few have ever been. Cherelle's mother has always been her protector and is determined to help her daughter to weather the storms of her life even if it means to revisit her past. The Water Ain't Blue Enough captures the issues of love, life, rejection and redemption.

Free to Fly | Various | $15 + Shipping

The inner strength of women that causes them to stand with confidence when their wings have been broken is beautiful. Free to Fly: Wisdom for the Seasons in a Woman's Life is a celebration of this strength. The contributors to this collection have opened their hearts to expose you to experiences that could have broken them yet they emerged Free to Fly with a testimony. These writings will provoke discussion, inspire you to dream and encourage you to ponder your own freedom.

Standing On Faith | Doris Miller | $14.95 + Shipping

When Doris Miller was a child she wondered about who made the earth and all of the things within it. She has come to recognize through the years that God was preparing her to be used by Him to help others believe in and have a greater faith in Him. In this book she tells her journey through faith, learning to be obedient and hearken to God's voice which she wants others to know how stand on faith.